THE CAPTAIN`S POLYGRAPH

By C. Hurchel Stagner

Order this book online at www.trafford.com/09-0426
or email orders@trafford.com

Most Trafford titles are also available at major online book retailers.

Note for Librarians: A cataloguing record for this book is available from Library and Archives Canada at www.collectionscanada.ca/amicus/index-e.html

ISBN: 978-1-4269-0310-6

www.trafford.com

North America & international
toll-free: 1 888 232 4444 (USA & Canada)
phone: 250 383 6864 ♦ fax: 250 383 6804
email: info@trafford.com

The United Kingdom & Europe
phone: +44 (0)1865 487 395 ♦ local rate: 0845 230 9601
facsimile: +44 (0)1865 481 507 ♦ email: info.uk@trafford.com

10 9 8 7 6 5 4 3 2 1

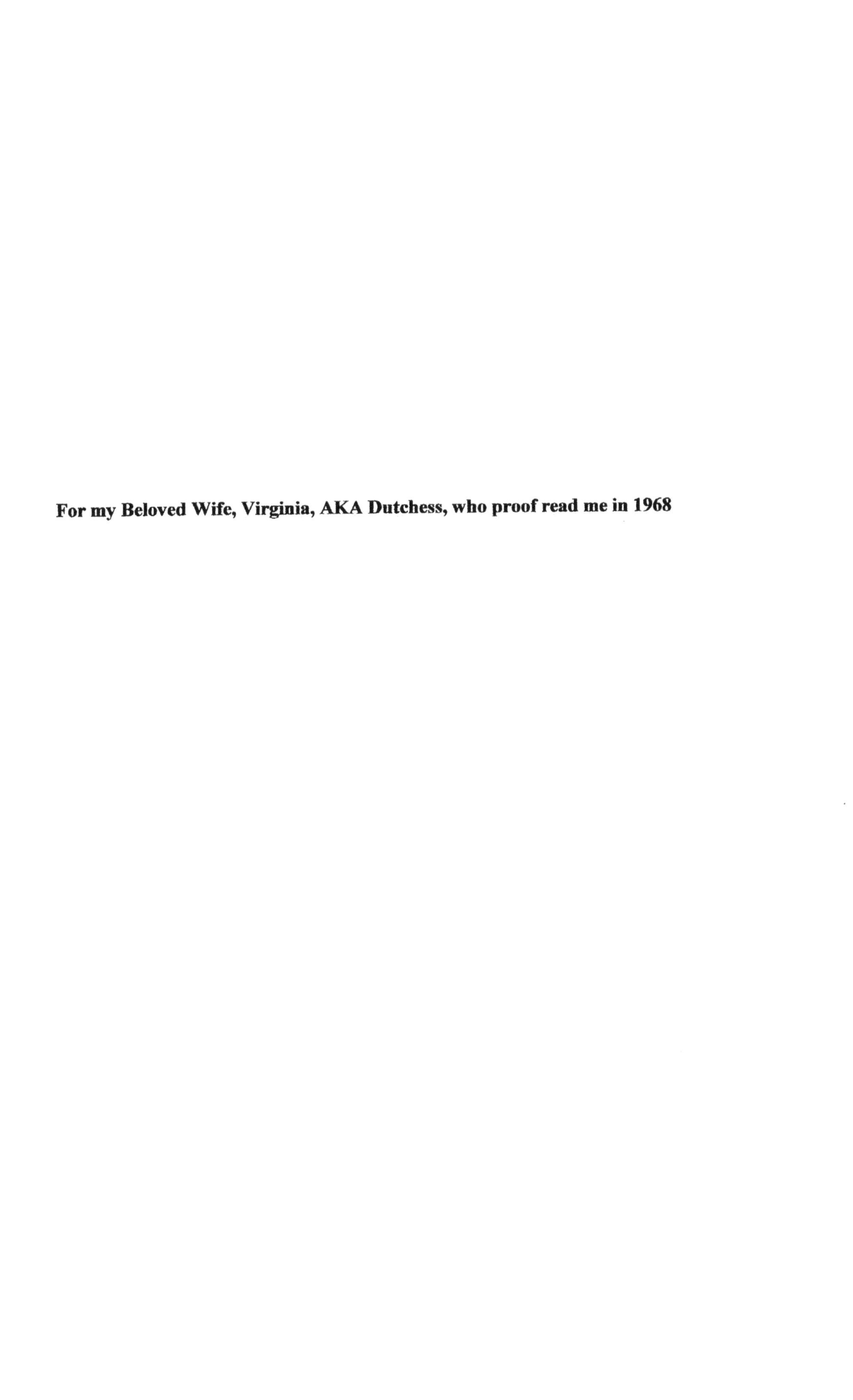

For my Beloved Wife, Virginia, AKA Dutchess, who proof read me in 1968

CONTENTS

PREFACE

NEVADA TEST SITE

On April 14,1962, at the Nevada Test Site referred to as NTS, Captain Clyde H. Stagner, a Signal Corp Captain, and a radiological monitor from the Reynolds Electric engineering Company, REECO, sat in their jeeps at a vantage point approximately 1,500 yards from the vertical face of a mesa. A nuclear device, officially named "EVENT PLATTE", was sealed in a closed horizontal tunnel dug into the mesa. This was a Department of Defense, DOD, scheduled event. After the detonation, the REECO monitor was scheduled to drive over to the mesa`s closed tunnel entrance and obtain a radiation level measurement. This result would enable a mathematical calculation for determination of a time for acceptable human reentry into the tunnel via digging. The detonation occurred at the designated time of 10 AM.

The instantaneous result was a plume of failed mode fallout blown horizontally outward toward Stagner and his companions who spontaneously traveled swiftly southward. Looking back, Stagner saw the coned plume being lifted upward and curled back over the top of the mesa. The location was in close proximity to the northern border of NTS. Stagner became concerned about the adverse impact on the unprotected, unwarned civilians located and the area of possible contamination outside the site boundary. He knew the United States Public Health Service, USPHS, had the official offsite safety task with the Atomic Energy Commission having the onsite safety task, "*this was a DOD nuclear event and he was the DOD Radiological Safety Officer. was he responsible and accountable without authority*".

Returning to Mercury, Nevada, Stagner and his companion located the USPHS in a Quonset. One individual was on a radio communicating with their fixed wing aircraft which was waggling its wings at two cowboys in an effort to get them out of the fallout. The remaining individual was at a typewriter faithfully logging, as best she could, the conversations and events as they occurred. There was no indication of a detailed constant azimuth, constant ground speed, constant elevation above ground level, and incremental time spaced radiation measurements. This was the aerial radiological survey standard procedure taught at the United States Army Chemical Corps School where Stagner was an instructor.

Upon returning to the Operations Section, Stagner consulted with the Ass`t Operations Officer concerning the necessity of including a comprehensive off site aerial radiological monitoring survey for the scheduled Small Boy Event, a surface burst with fallout. He explained the need for obtaining the radiological data as necessary for the evaluation of possible protective and treatment requirements for the off site populace. An alternative safety measure was an evacuation of a large area of Nevada.

A couple of weeks later, the Ass`t Operations Officer informed Stagner that the Chemical Corps did not teach radiological monitoring according to a Colonel of the Chemical Corps stationed at Sandia Base. Stagner`s request for monitoring was

denied, "*someone in this organization at Sandia Base does not want, or has been advised to refrain from, detailed off site radiological monitoring for the civilian population*".

Capt. Stagner requested to be relieved as the DOD Rad-Safe Officer for nuclear testing. His request was granted and he returned to Fort McClellan in May, 1962. During his tenure at NTS, Stagner developed a great respect and admiration for Lt. Col. Harry Elmendorf, United States Air Force, Operations Officer for Weapons Effects and Tests.

Germany 1955

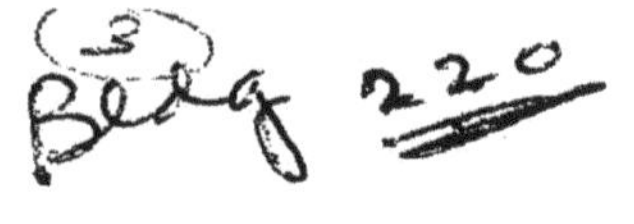

HEADQUARTERS
U. S. ARMY CHEMICAL CORPS TRAINING COMMAND
FORT MCCLELLAN, ALABAMA

SPECIAL ORDERS
NUMBER 56

EXTRACT

14 March 1962

1. TC 201. Indiv this station placed on TDY as indic. Rtn proper station upon completion of TDY. TDN.

STAGNER, CLYDE H 065183 CAPT CmlC USA CmlC School
TDY to: Sandia Base, New Mexico
WP date: OA 15 March 1962
Pd: Approx 90 days
Scty Clnc: TOP SECRET
Purpose: Radiological Safety Planning
Auth: CCR 55-2 and AR 310-10
Acct Clas: 2122020 04-3242 P2100-21 (2110.1211) S01-088 BVN 1211-131
Sp Instr: Commercial Air/Rail/TPA/If requested TO will furnish necessary transportation. Travel time in excess of travel by CC WB chargeable as leave. 5 DDALV prior to TDY. CIPAP. Off will rpt NLT 21 March 1962.

FOR THE COMMANDER:

OFFICIAL:

GARY K. COWELL
2d Lt, CmlC
Asst Adjutant

THOMAS C. NELSON
Captain, AGC
Adjutant

DISTRIBUTION: G

AND CIVILIAN PERSONNEL TDY AND PCS TRAVEL
(AR 310-10 and CPR T-3)

1. TYPE OF TRAVEL ORDERS
[X] TDY. UCMR PROPER STA. [ ] PCS *(Civilian only)* [ ] CONFIRMATORY ORDERS

2. NAME OF REQUESTING OFFICE	3. TELEPHONE EXT.	4. DATE
Deputy Chief of Staff, Weapons Effects & Tests Group	52114	22 Mar 62

5. FIRST NAME - MIDDLE INITIAL - LAST NAME	GRADE	SERVICE NUMBER	ARM OR SERVICE *(Military)* POSITION OR TITLE *(Civilian)*	SECURITY CLEARANCE
CLYDE H. STAGNER	CAPTAIN	065183	USA	TS

6. ORGANIZATION AND STATION
USA Element, Sandia Base, New Mexico

7. TO PROCEED O/A
24 Mar 62

8. APPROXIMATE NUMBER OF DAYS
90

9. ITINERARY [X] CIPAP
From: Sandia Base, New Mexico to Nevada Test Site, Mercury, Nevada and return.

10. PURPOSE OF TEMPORARY DUTY To man DOD Test Organization and to participate in such test operations and planning as required.

11. TRANSPORTATION AUTHORIZED
[X] COMMON CARRIER: [X] AIR [X] SURFACE [ ] WATER [ ] AS DETERMINED BY TRANSPORTATION OFF. *(Military only)*
[X] GOVERNMENT OWNED: [X] VEHICLE [X] AIRCRAFT [ ] VESSEL
[X] PRIVATELY-OWNED VEHICLE AT RATE OF____ CENTS PER MILE [ ] TPA-TMDAG
[ ] REIMBURSEMENT LIMITED TO COST TO GOVT OF TRAVEL BY USUAL MODE OF TRANSPORTATION, INCLUDING PER DIEM. *(Civilian only)*

12. PER DIEM AUTHORIZED *(Civilian Personnel only)*
[ ] MAXIMUM AUTHORIZED BY CPR T-3 [ ] OTHER RATES OF PER DIEM *(Specify)*

13. TRANSPORTATION OF DEPENDENTS *(Civilian Personnel only)*
[ ] EMPLOYEE REQUESTS TRANSPORTATION OF DEPENDENTS WHOSE NAME(S) AGE(S) AND RELATIONSHIP(S) APPEAR UNDER REMARKS
[ ] TRANSPORTATION AUTHORIZED BY GOVERNMENT [ ] VEHICLE [ ] AIRCRAFT [ ] VESSEL
[ ] TRANSPORTATION AUTHORIZED BY COMMON CARRIER *(Commercial Air, Rail, Bus, Vessel)*
[ ] TRANSPORTATION AUTHORIZED BY PRIVATELY-OWNED CONVEYANCE

14. SHIPMENT OF HOUSEHOLD GOODS *(Civilian personnel only)*
[ ] EMPLOYEE HAS DEPENDENTS AND IS AUTHORIZED MOVEMENT OF HOUSEHOLD GOODS NOT IN EXCESS OF 7000 POUNDS NET WEIGHT
[ ] EMPLOYEE DOES NOT HAVE DEPENDENTS AND IS AUTHORIZED MOVEMENT OF HOUSEHOLD GOODS NOT IN EXCESS OF 2500 POUNDS NET WEIGHT

15. REMARKS *(Use this space for special requirements, delay, authority for issuance, names of dependents, designation as courier, superior accommodations, excess baggage, etc.)*

FCWT Security will make visit announcement, if necessary.

Officer authorized to have in possession classified material up to and including SECRET RESTRICTED DATA.

Government quarters available, Government mess not available at Nevada Test Site, Mercury, Nevada.

Commercial air to include jet (tourist).

Transp. $ 74.40
P/D 540.00
TOTAL 614.40

16. ADMINISTRATIVE APPROVAL
WILLIAM J. McCARTHY, 2D LT, AGC, USA
Asst Admin & Pers Officer, FCWT
(Name, grade or title)

17. FISCAL APPROVAL *(Chargeable to)*
TDN 21X2040 210-7844 P5910-21-22 S29-044
CMS 25XXXM4

NAME, GRADE OR TITLE
H.G. BERKSHIRE, LT COL, FC F&AO

FOR USE OF APPROVING OFFICE ONLY

18. AGENCY
HEADQUARTERS FIELD COMMAND, DASA

19. ORDER NUMBER/REFERENCE
LO WT 216

20. DATE
23 Mar 62

21. APPROVED. TRAVEL TO BE PERFORMED IS NECESSARY IN THE PUBLIC SERVICE. WP.
AUTH: Ltr, CHDASA, DASAAG 210 .4, Subj: Delegation of Authority to Issue Travel Orders, 19 May 60, and DOD Directive 5158.2, 2 Feb 60.
FOR THE COMMANDER:

NAME, GRADE OR TITLE
WILLIAM J. McCARTHY, 2d Lt, USA, Asst Adj Gen

DA FORM 662 1 OCT 61 PREVIOUS EDITIONS ARE OBSOLETE. 1

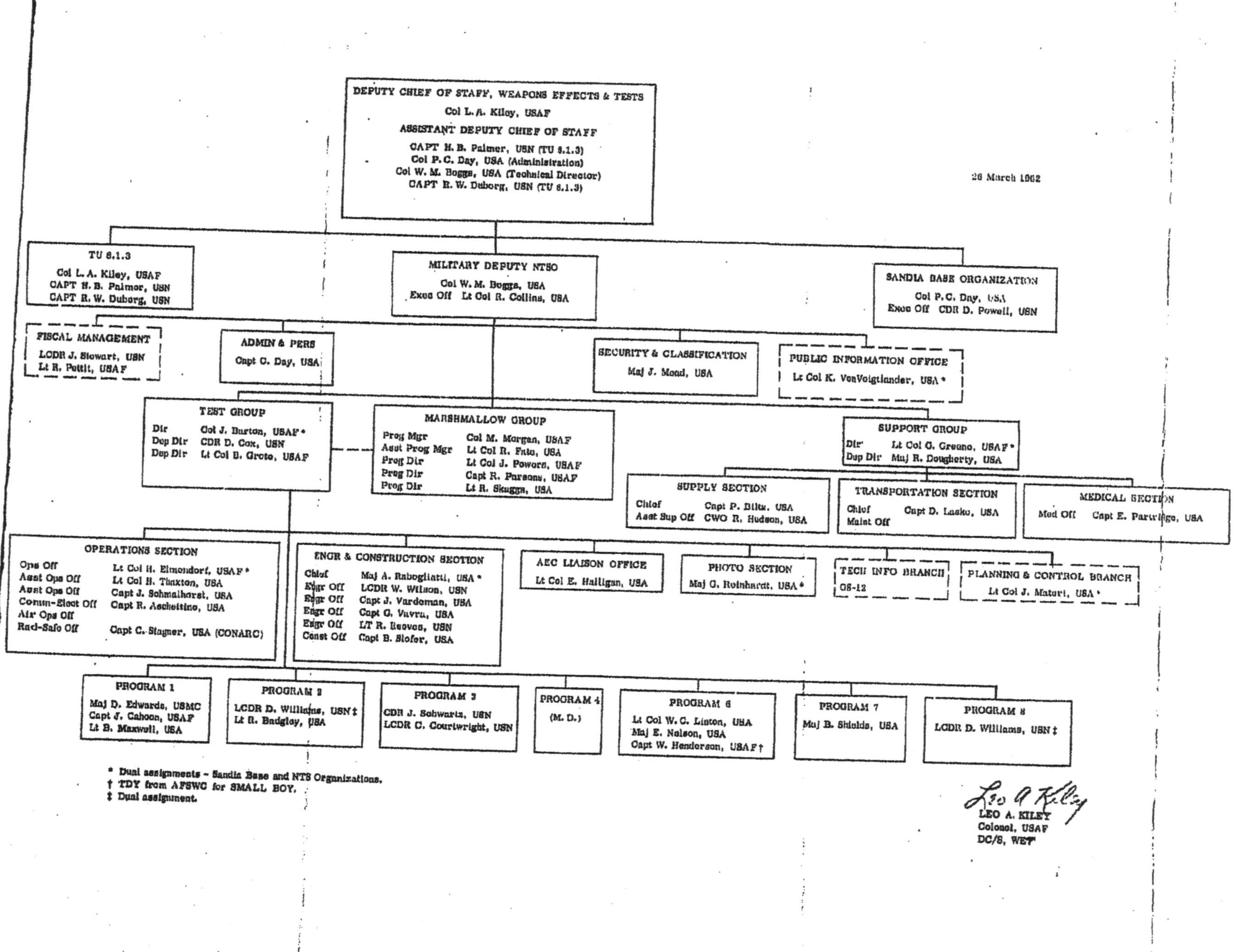
DEPUTY CHIEF OF STAFF, WEAPONS EFFECTS & TESTS
Col L. A. Kiley, USAF
ASSISTANT DEPUTY CHIEF OF STAFF
CAPT H. B. Palmer, USN (TU 8.1.3)
Col P. C. Day, USA (Administration)
Col W. M. Boggs, USA (Technical Director)
CAPT R. W. Duborg, USN (TU 8.1.3)
26 March 1962
TU 8.1.3
Col L. A. Kiley, USAF
CAPT H. B. Palmer, USN
CAPT R. W. Duborg, USN
MILITARY DEPUTY NTSO
Col W. M. Boggs, USA
Exec Off Lt Col R. Collins, USA
SANDIA BASE ORGANIZATION
Col P. C. Day, USA
Exec Off CDR D. Powell, USN
FISCAL MANAGEMENT
LCDR J. Stewart, USN
Lt R. Pettit, USAF
ADMIN & PERS
Capt C. Day, USA
SECURITY & CLASSIFICATION
Maj J. Mead, USA
PUBLIC INFORMATION OFFICE
Lt Col K. VonVoigtlander, USA *
TEST GROUP
Dir Col J. Barton, USAF *
Dep Dir CDR D. Cox, USN
Dep Dir Lt Col B. Grote, USAF
MARSHMALLOW GROUP
Prog Mgr Col M. Morgan, USAF
Asst Prog Mgr Lt Col R. Fato, USA
Prog Dir Lt Col J. Powers, USAF
Prog Dir Capt R. Parsons, USAF
Prog Dir Lt R. Skaggs, USA
SUPPORT GROUP
Dir Lt Col G. Greene, USAF *
Dep Dir Maj R. Dougherty, USA
SUPPLY SECTION
Chief Capt P. Biltz, USA
Asst Sup Off CWO R. Hudson, USA
TRANSPORTATION SECTION
Chief Capt D. Lasko, USA
Maint Off
MEDICAL SECTION
Med Off Capt E. Partridge, USA
OPERATIONS SECTION
Ops Off Lt Col H. Elmendorf, USAF *
Asst Ops Off Lt Col H. Thaxton, USA
Asst Ops Off Capt J. Schmalhorst, USA
Comm-Elect Off Capt R. Aschettino, USA
Air Ops Off
Rad-Safe Off Capt C. Slagner, USA (CONARC)
ENGR & CONSTRUCTION SECTION
Chief Maj A. Raboglliatti, USA *
Engr Off LCDR W. Wilson, USN
Engr Off Capt J. Vardeman, USA
Engr Off Capt G. Vavra, USA
Engr Off LT R. Reeves, USN
Const Off Capt B. Slofer, USA
AEC LIAISON OFFICE
Lt Col E. Halligan, USA
PHOTO SECTION
Maj G. Reinhardt, USA *
TECH INFO BRANCH
OS-12
PLANNING & CONTROL BRANCH
Lt Col J. Maturi, USA *
PROGRAM 1
Maj D. Edwards, USMC
Capt J. Cahoon, USAF
Lt B. Maxwell, USA
PROGRAM 2
LCDR D. Williams, USN ‡
Lt R. Badgley, USA
PROGRAM 3
CDR J. Schwartz, USN
LCDR C. Courtwright, USN
PROGRAM 4
(M. D.)
PROGRAM 6
Lt Col W. C. Linton, USA
Maj E. Nelson, USA
Capt W. Henderson, USAF †
PROGRAM 7
Maj B. Shields, USA
PROGRAM 8
LCDR D. Williams, USN ‡
* Dual assignments - Sandia Base and NTS Organizations.
† TDY from AFSWC for SMALL BOY.
‡ Dual assignment.
LEO A. KILEY
Colonel, USAF
DC/S, WET

APPENDIX B (continued)

ANNOUNCED UNITED STATES NUCLEAR TESTS - BY EVENT NAME

EVENT NAME	DATE (GCT)	LOCATION	TYPE	PURPOSE	YIELD RANGE
PIN STRIPE	04/25/66	NTS	SHAFT	WEAPONS EFFECTS	LESS THAN 20KT
DOD EVENT. MINOR LEVELS OF RADIOACTIVITY DETECTED OFF SITE					
PINE	07/26/58	ENEWETAK	BARGE	WEAPONS RELATED	
PINEAU	07/16/81	NTS	SHAFT	WEAPONS RELATED	LESS THAN 20 KT
PIPEFISH	04/29/64	NTS	SHAFT	WEAPONS RELATED	LESS THAN 20KT
MINOR LEVELS OF RADIOACTIVITY DETECTED ON-SITE ONLY					
PIPKIN	10/08/69	NTS	SHAFT	WEAPONS RELATED	200 TO 1000KT
PIRANHA	05/13/66	NTS	SHAFT	WEAPONS RELATED	20 TO 200KT
PISONIA	07/17/58	ENEWETAK	BARGE	WEAPONS RELATED	
PLAID II	02/03/66	NTS	SHAFT	WEAPONS RELATED	LESS THAN 20KT
MINOR LEVELS OF RADIOACTIVITY DETECTED ON-SITE ONLY					
PLATTE	04/14/62	NTS	TUNNEL	WEAPONS RELATED	1.85KT
RELEASE OF RADIOACTIVITY DETECTED OFF SITE					
PLATYPUS	02/24/62	NTS	SHAFT	WEAPONS RELATED	LOW
MINOR LEVELS OF RADIOACTIVITY DETECTED ON-SITE ONLY					
PLEASANT	05/29/63	NTS	SHAFT	WEAPONS RELATED	LOW
MINOR LEVELS OF RADIOACTIVITY DETECTED ON-SITE ONLY					
PLIERS	08/27/69	NTS	SHAFT	WEAPONS RELATED	LESS THAN 20KT
MINOR LEVELS OF RADIOACTIVITY DETECTED ON-SITE ONLY					
POD	10/29/69	NTS	SHAFT	WEAPONS RELATED	20 TO 200KT
MINOR LEVELS OF RADIOACTIVITY DETECTED OFFSITE					
POMMARD	03/14/68	NTS	SHAFT	WEAPONS RELATED	1.5KT
POOL	03/17/76	NTS	SHAFT	WEAPONS RELATED	200 TO 500KT
POPLAR	07/12/58	BIKINI	BARGE	WEAPONS RELATED	
PORTMANTEAU	08/30/74	NTS	SHAFT	WEAPONS RELATED	20 TO 200KT
PORTULACA	06/28/73	NTS	SHAFT	WEAPONS RELATED	20 TO 200KT
POST	04/09/55	NTS	TOWER	WEAPONS RELATED	2KT
PRISCILLA	06/24/57	NTS	BALLOON	WEAPONS RELATED	37KT
PROJECT 56 NO 1	11/01/55	NTS	SURFACE	SAFETY EXPER.	ZERO
PROJECT 56 NO 2	11/03/55	NTS	SURFACE	SAFETY EXPER.	ZERO
PU DISPERSAL.					

Test:	**HUDSON**		
Date:	04/12/62	**Sponsor:**	LRL
Time:	1000 PST	**Depth of Burial:**	480 ft
Location:	NTS U9n	**Purpose:**	Weapons Related
Type:	Shaft	**Yield:**	Low
Release Detected:	Onsite Only	**Type of Release:**	Drillback

Drillback Release Activity at Time of Release, in Curies: 5.0×10^2

^{133}Xe and ^{135}Xe in curies: 5.0×10^2

Release Summary: A drillback release occurred from a postshot drill hole on April 16, 1962, and lasted for eight hours.

References: (A) (C) (E) (F) (H) (AY) (DA)

Test:	**PLATTE**		
Date:	04/14/62	**Sponsor:**	LRL
Time:	1000 PST	**Depth of Burial:**	560 ft
Location:	NTS U12k.01	**Purpose:**	Weapons Related
Type:	Tunnel	**Yield:**	1.85 kt
Release Detected:	Offsite	**Type of Release:**	Test and Test/Prompt Particle Sampling

Test Release at R+12 Hours, in Curies: 1.9×10^6

Isotopes Identified in the Release: ^{40}K, ^{95}Zr/^{95}Nb, ^{103}Ru, ^{105}Ru, ^{131}I, ^{133}I, ^{135}I, ^{132}Te, ^{140}Ba/^{140}La, ^{141}Ce, and ^{144}Ce

Cloud Direction: Northerly over Highway 25 (Nevada) at a bearing of approximately 20 degrees

Maximum Activity Detected in Air Offsite: 34,000 picocuries of gross beta activity per cubic meter of air at Queen City Summit, Nevada (unpopulated)

Maximum Gamma Exposure Rate Detected Offsite: 47 mR/h at Queen City Summit, Nevada

Maximum Iodine Level Detected Offsite: 3,500 picocuries of ^{131}I per cubic meter of air, 23,000 picocuries of ^{133}I per cubic meter of air, and 37,000 picocuries of ^{135}I per cubic meter of air at Queen City Summit, Nevada

Maximum Distance Radiation Detected Offsite: 0.10 mR/h at 28.1 miles northeast of Currant, Nevada

REYNOLDS ELECTRICAL & ENGINEERING CO., Inc.
Electrical Construction Engineers

SANTA FE · EL PASO · HOUSTON · ALBUQUERQUE · LAS VEGAS · ATLANTA · OMAHA

SUBJECT: Tunnel Re-entry Course

DATE: APR 2 6 1962
NTS-8018-H

REPLY TO: AEC Contract Office, P.O. Box 371, Las Vegas, Nevada

Clyde H. Stagner
Captain, USA
DOD Rad-Safe Officer
Quonset 32
Mercury, Nevada

Dear Sir:

We are transmitting herewith an outline of a suggested course concerning potential hazards and re-entry procedures to underground nuclear detonation sites. It appears that a one day course should be sufficient to orient and familiarize staff military officers with information required for planning purposes.

TUNNEL RE-ENTRY COURSE

TIME	EVENT
0800 - 0830	Travel to CP-2
0830 - 0930	Underground Nuclear Explosion Phenomena and Experience
0930 - 0945	Coffee Break
0945 - 1045	Toxic Materials Hazards
1045 - 1145	Radiation Hazards
1145 - 1215	Lunch
1215 - 1315	Mine Rescue Principles
1315 - 1415	Re-entry Team Organization and Functions

APR 2 6 1962

Clyde H. Stagner, Captain
Page 2

NTS-8018-H

1415 - 1445	Travel to Tunnel "A"
1445 - 1545	Tunnel Re-entry Exercise
1545 - 1615	Travel to CP-2
1615 - 1645	Critique
1645 - 1715	Travel to Mercury

It is suggested that no more than 25 personnel be assigned to each class. Conduct of this class would require coordination and liaison with several agencies. Our Division could organize and sponsor the course if approval is received from AEC-NOO.

If we can be of further assistance, please call on us.

Very truly yours,

REYNOLDS ELECTRICAL & ENGINEERING CO., INC.

Floyd W. Wilcox

FWW:vm

Table 5. Dose rates measured off site during surveillance of the Platte event.

AZIMUTH (°)	DISTANCE (mile)	LOCATION	CLOCK TIME PST	DOSE RATE (net mr/hr) γ	β + γ
			4/14/62		
		On Valley Road, N of the Gunnery Range Boundary			
32	31	.1 mi.	1410	0.02	
		.3 mi. (from Boundary)	1140	Zero	
		"	1145	0.01	
	32	.5 mi.	1411	0.04	
36	33	3.1 mi.	1416	0.01	
42	36	12.6 mi.	1439	0.02	
36	33	At Kawich Valley Turn-off	1215	1.5	
		On Valley Road, W of Kawich Valley Turn-off			
36	33	.3 mi.	1217	1.5	
35		.7 mi. (from Turn-off)	1220	3.0	
		.8 mi.	1225	5.0	
34	36	At Gunderson's Ranch in Penoyer Valley (8 readings)	1030-1210	All Zero	
			1215	0.03	
			1218	0.09	
			1220	0.19	
			1222	1.5	
			1224	0.25	
			1228	0.08	
			1232	0.30	
			1235	0.03	
			1240	0.03	
			1245	0.16	
			1250	0.41	
			1255	1.0	
			1300	0.09	
			1345	0.02	
			1400	0.35	
			1410	0.01	
			1420	0.01	
			1430	0.02	
			1440	0.06	
			1500	0.09	
			1505	0.09	
			1515	0.05	
			1520	0.05	
			1540	0.14	
			1600	0.03	
			1715	Zero	
			1743	Zero	
21	40	At Queen City Summit (3 readings)	1005-1100	All Zero	
			1217	1.6	
			1220	1.4	

by FOIA

Table 5. Dose rates measured off site during surveillance of the Platte event. (cont'd.)

AZIMUTH (°)	DISTANCE (mile)	LOCATION	CLOCK TIME PST	DOSE RATE (net mr/hr) γ	β + γ
21	40	At Queen City Summit (Cont.)			
			1244	42	
			1251	47	
			1330	6	
			1447	1.3	
			1458	0.5	
			1550	1.1	
			1600	1.9	
			1723	0.7	
		On Hwy. 25, going SE from Queen City Summit			
22	39	.5 mi.	1252	45	65
		.8 mi. (from Queen City	1436	0.05	13
		1 mi. Summit)	1254	45	68
		"	1450	1.5	
23		1.5 mi.	1257	45	70
		2 mi.	1259	42	61
		"	1451	1.2	
		"	1522	0.5	
		2.5 mi.	1303	32	55
24		2.8 mi.	1434	1.0	
		3 mi.	1304	30	50
		"	1453	1.2	
		"	1527	0.3	
		"	1645	0.05	
		3.5 mi.	1306	22	42
25		4 mi.	1308	18	36
		"	1325	2.8	4.3
		"	1335	0.2	
		"	1415	Zero	
		"	1455	0.9	
		"	1500	0.9	
		"	1645	0.05	
		4.5 mi.	1310	12	24
26		4.8 mi.	1432	0.4	
		5 mi.	1312	8	22
		"	1330	0.6	1.4
		"	1338	Zero	
		5.5 mi.	1314	9	15
		"	1527	0.05	
27		5.8 mi.	1431	0.1	
28		6 mi.	1315	7	14
		"	1335	0.6	1.0
		"	1444	Zero	0.05
29		6.5 mi.	1317	2	11
		"	1320	7	14
30		6.8 mi.	1430	Zero	
		7 mi.	1430	0.6	1.0
		7.1 mi.	1312	0.90	
		"	1315	0.05	
32		8 mi.	1432	0.6	1.0
33		9 mi.	1434	0.05	0.3
34		10 mi.	1427	0.16	
		"	1437	0.05	0.1

by FOIA

Table 5. Dose rates measured off site during surveillance of the Platte event. (cont'd.)

AZIMUTH (°)	DISTANCE (mile)	LOCATION	CLOCK TIME PST	DOSE RATE (net mr/hr) γ	β + γ
		On Hwy. 25, going SE from Queen City Summit (Cont.)			
34	39	10 mi.	1440	0.05	0.1
		" (from Queen	1524	0.6	
		10.2 mi. City Summit)	1347	Zero	
36		11 mi.	1345	Zero	
38		12 mi.	1315	Zero	
		"	1343	Zero	
40		13 mi.	1342	Zero	0.05
		"	1446	Zero	
41		14 mi.	1340	Zero	
		"	1410	Zero	
		"	1444	0.11	
		"	1445	0.09	
		"	1448	Zero	
		"	1635	0.02	
		"	1635	0.02	
42		15 mi.	1450	Zero	Zero
44	38	16 mi.	1453	Zero	Zero
		"	1453	Zero	Zero
46	38	At Coyote Summit (3 readings)	1455-1505	All Zero	All Zero
57	39	On Hwy. 25, 7 miles SE of Coyote Summit	1510	Zero	
		On Hwy. 25, going NW from Queen City Summit			
20	40	1 mi.	1500	Zero	
14	42	5.4 mi. (from Queen	1712	0.7	
		5.5 mi. City Summit)	1215	0.09	
12		6.5 mi.	1217	0.34	
10	43	7.5 mi.	1219	0.03	
		"	1708	0.6	
7	51	At Diablo	1100	Zero	
			1145	Zero	
			1225	Zero	
			1230	Zero	
			1231	0.01	
			1234	0.09	
			1235	0.3	
			1236	0.5	
			1237	0.7	
			1238	1.0	
			1239	1.0	
			1243	0.7	
			1244	1.5	
			1245	1.6	
			1246	0.9	
			1247	1.4	

Table 5. Dose rates measured off site during surveillance of the Platte event. (cont'd.)

AZIMUTH (°)	DISTANCE (mile)	LOCATION	CLOCK TIME PST	DOSE RATE (net mr/hr) γ	β + γ
7	51	At Diablo (Cont.)	1248	1.8	
			1252	1.9	
			1254	2.0	
			1258	1.5	
			1301	0.8	
			1305	1.4	
			1307	1.6	
			1308	3.0	
			1309	3.5	
			1310	4.0	
			1311	4.9	
			1314	7.0	
			1317	3.5	
			1320	2.0	
			1322	1.5	
			1329	1.2	
			1333	1.2	
			1338	1.1	
			1342	1.0	
			1347	1.2	
			1355	1.2	
			1400	1.2	
			1410	1.0	
			1415	0.2	
			1650	1.5	
		On Hwy. 25, N of Diablo			
5	60	10 mi.	1420	0.5	
0	69	22 mi.	1430	Zero	
3	66	At the Jct. of Hwy. 25 & the road to Nyala	1420	0.28	
			1425	0.13	
			1435	0.04	
0	69	At Twin Springs Ranch (13 readings)	1140-1430	All Zero	
351	71	At Warm Springs	1100	Zero	
			1500	Zero	
		On the road to Queen City Pond, NE of Hwy. 25			
22	40	1 mi.	1503	1.0	
	41	2 mi. (from Hwy. 25)	1505	1.15	
21	42	3 mi.	1510	1.35	
20	43	4 mi.	1515	1.3	
		On Sand Spring Road, NE of Hwy. 25			
32	40	1 mi.	1300	10	
		2 mi.	1532	0.3	

by FOIA

3439 Bradley Place
Raleigh, North Carolina
27 March 1962

Dear Clyde:

As much as I hate to be a bother, I am muchly afraid I must. I need as much data as you can furnish about all the attenuation studies you have accomplished with those vacuum tubes, including any new poop you may have gatered since I left. It appears we have struck a nerve here in one particular area, and it may vastly aid our defense posture.

Several of the profs here are working for Uncle Sam in development of ion-propulsion sustems for space vehicles. In this regard they anticipate triggering the assembly with a gamma source some distance away. I have been discussing this with Dean Menius of the Department of Physical Sciences and Applied Mathematics. We were talking in particular about the nature and oscillations of plasma systems, and I at one point mentioned the studies you had made on gamma attenuation. He immediately became frantic for more information. I gave him some of our data (about twenty some cases was all I could locate in my files), and now he has called me four times today to get him more, and even suggested at one point a phone call. I was sure I could explain the situation more fully in this letter.

If the attenuation in electron fields is as much as was indicated in a few of your cases, and there is reason to believe the electron density in this system will be as great or greater than in the vacuum tube, then it will require that they change the size of their gamma "trigger" substantially in this application.

Much of the information is currently classified, and also as yet unpublished. If this is of any help to them, the source may be quoted in the literature, and thus some recognition of the idea may be obtained. At any rate, it may prod them into an investigation of the nature we suggested in the Blue Sky suggestion, if not for people, at least for space travel.

I am as busy as I can be, taking 15 semester hours and also three labs and my research. Not much time for loafing here. Once in a while I even get to see my family, e.g. on every other Sunday afternoon! This will continue until next fall late, after my preliminary exams, then will ease somewhat as I go into nothing but research. What an opportunity!

I will certainly appreciate as quick a supply of this information as you can give me, realizing that you must of course assemble it. It will be supremely useful.

Ran out of space! I'm the world's worst typist. Kindest regards to all. Say Hi for me to Col's Kontra & Colgin. Sincerely, Curley

Our best to, your family. Ed

Capt Stagner

HEADQUARTERS
DEPARTMENT OF DEFENSE TEST ORGANIZATION
Field Command, Defense Atomic Support Agency
Post Office Box 207, Mercury, Nevada

23 April 1962

MEMORANDUM FOR RECORD:

SUBJECT: SMALL BOY, Project 2.9 Manned Stations

TO: DOD Test Group Director
Nevada Test Site
Mercury, Nevada

1. A conference was conducted on 19 April 1962 at 1030 hours in Quonset 32, DOD Compound, with the following personnel present:

Captain Partridge, MD, Support Group
2/Lt Badgely, Program 2
Captain Stagner, DOD Rad Safety Officer

2. The following items with reference to personnel for manned stations of Project 2.9 were discussed and concurred in by all personnel.

a. Captain Partridge will review the medical records of the personnel and will interview each individual and conduct a physical examination approximately 2 to 3 weeks prior to the event and immediately prior to occupancy of manned stations.

b. Manned station personnel should be volunteers and well briefed prior to the event.

c. Each manned station to have an operational SOP for use within the station during occupancy.

d. "C" Rations are acceptable for use during occupancy of manned stations.

e. Blankets or warm clothing is necessary for warmth during night hours.

f. Captain Partridge will ascertain the adequacy of training of each individual (for each station) trained in first aid.

g. Captain Partridge will provide medical support to the Forward Control Point.

h. Captain Partridge will examine each individual upon his egress

23 April 1962

MEMORANDUM FOR RECORD: SUBJECT: SMALL BOY, Project 2.9 Manned Stations

from the manned station.

i. Eighteen year old individuals, or younger, will be precluded from participating in occupancy of manned stations.

j. Captain Partridge will notify the DOD Rad Safety Officer of any individual who, from a medical opinion, should not occupy a manned station.

k. Captain Partridge will forward a general report prior to the event and an after action report subsequent to the event to the DOD Rad Safety Officer.

3. Direct coordination will be effected between Lt Badgely and Captain Partridge to accomplish the applicable actions cited in paragraph 2, supra.

4. Captain Partridge will accomplish the liaison necessary to obtain assistance as required from REECo.

5. If additional requirements are deemed necessary by medical opinion, Captain Partridge will so inform the DOD Rad Safety Officer.

Clyde H. Stagner

CLYDE H. STAGNER
Captain, USA
DOD Rad Safety Officer

Copy to:
DOD Test Opns

DISTRIBUTION:
Prog Manager, SMALL BOY
Prog 2
DOD Test Opns
DOD Support Gp (Capt Partridge)
DOD Rad-Safe (Capt Stagner)

Maximum Iodine Level Detected Offsite: 500 picocuries of 131 I per cubic meter of air, 920 picocuries of 133 I, per cubic meter of air, and 2,300 picocuries of 135 I per cubic meter of air at Twin Springs, Nevada
Maximum Distance Radiation Detected Offsite: 3.0 mR/h at 11 miles northeast of Lockes, Nevada
Release Summary: A persistent cloud containing appreciable quantities of radioactivity, including particulates, was produced during the cratering process.
Detonation of this test resulted in the formation of a radioactive cloud that moved north from the test site. This cloud split into two portions. The lower portion traveled slightly west of north to the area of Highway 6 between Tonopah and Warm Springs, Nevada, then traveled east of north after assuming a width of 25-30 miles; the higher portion, above 11,000 ft mean sea level (MSL), traveled east of north.

References: (A) (E) (F) (AR) (GK)

Test: SMALL BOY

Date: 07/14/62
Time: 1130 PDT
Location: **NTS** Area 5
Type: Tower Yield: Low
Release Type of Detected: Offsite
Test Release: Atmospheric
Sponsor: DoD
Depth of Burial: 10 ft above ground
Purpose: Weapons Effects
Release: Test/Surface
Isotopes Identified in the Release: 95 Zr/95 Nb, 103 Ru, 131 I, 132 Te, and 140 Ba/140 La
Cloud Direction: Northeasterly
Maximum Activity Detected in Air Offsite: 140,000 picocuries of gross beta activity per cubic meter of air at Elko, Nevada
Maximum Gamma Exposure Rate Detected Offsite: 14 mR/h at 13 miles south of Alamo, Nevada
Maximum Iodine Level Detected Offsite: 1,100 picocuries of 131 I per cubic meter of air at Caliente, Nevada, and 3,500 picocuries of 131 I per liter in milk at Caliente, Nevada
Maximum Distance Radiation Detected Offsite: 0.02 mR/h at seven miles south of Parowan, Utah, on Highway 143
Release Summary: This test resulted in the formation of a radioactive cloud that moved east from surface ground zero and crossed Highway 93 south of Alamo, Nevada. During the night of July 14 and the morning of July 15, the cloud moved further east into Utah, and it reached such low levels that it was detected only in **small** segments by ground monitoring.
References: (A) (E) (F) (AR) (GL)

Test: BANDICOOT

Date: 10/19/62
Time: 1100 PDT
Location: **NTS** U3bj
Type: Shaft
Release Type of Detected: Offsite
Test Release at R+12 Hours, in Curies: 3.0 x 10 6
Sponsor: LASL
Depth of Burial: 800 ft
Purpose: Weapons Related
Yield: 12.5 kt
Release: Test
Isotopes Identified in the Release: 95 Zr/95 Nb, 103 Ru, 131 I, 133 I, 135 I, 132 Te, and 140 Ba/140 La
Cloud Direction: Northerly for the lower part of the cloud, south southwesterly for the upper portion of the cloud
Maximum Activity Detected in Air Offsite: 52,000 picocuries of gross beta activity per cubic meter of air at Death Valley Junction, California
Maximum Gamma Exposure Rate Detected Offsite: Greater than 20 mR/h on Highway 95,

CHAPTER 1

RESOLUTION

The cool evening air was calm on a November night in 1962 as Captain Stagner made his way through the entrance and foyer of the Fort McClellan Officers Club. A posted notice indicated the direction and room number for the meeting of John C Calhoun Chapter # 343 of the National Sojourners, Inc. Entering the room,greetings were exchanged with other officers and warrant officers: membership was limited to these ranks held past or present.. Several members present were reserve officers and warrant officers from local Alabama military reserve units.

Reserve Warrant Officer "Woody" Woodruff was a car salesman in Anniston, Alabama. "Woody" had assisted and arranged for Captain Stagner` s stepson to join the De Molay in Anniston where he gave the beautiful Mother` s Day presentation in the spring of 1961. Major Amos Johnson was Capt Stagner` s next door neighbor on Avery Drive in Fort McClellan. Lt Col. Austin was the executive Officer of the fort` s Noble Army Hospital. Another twenty members were seated at the long table dividing the room when Col. Dozier, Commanding Officer, 100th Chemical Group, and Chapter President, entered. After the door was secured, the President called the meeting to order. Following Robert` s Rules of Order, the meeting proceeded routinely until new business was called whereupon Col. Dozier rose and stated there was a Resolution to be presented for membership approval.

After the resolution reading which cited the failure of President Kennedy to provide air cover for the Bay of Pigs Cuban invasion and other failures, the resolution called for joining with other organizations to oppose President Kennedy. The resolution did not list the "other organizations" or the protocol for opposition to President Kennedy. Stagner mulled *"the Hatch Act prohibited military officer participation in certain political activities- the proposed opposition violated his presidential appointment as an officer in the regular U.S. Army - the proposed action was the antithesis of the 10th Masonic degree to which he firmly subscribed"*. The Captain obtained the floor, rose and adamantly expressed opposition to the resolution opposing the Commander-in-Chief. After a moment of dead silence, Warrant Officer Woodruff looked up and disdainfully uttered, "Are not you against a leftist dictator taking over this country?"

Captain Stagner, looking down on the seated Woodruff, responded emphatically with, "I am against a dictator taking over this country whether from the left -or the right!"

Silence again ensued until someone at the end of the table moved for adjournment. The motion was quickly seconded and followed by Col. Dozier` s gentle tap of the gavel concurrently with a low voiced, "This meeting is adjourned". Members silently filed out of the room with most continuing to exit the Officers Club. Usually, most in attendance reassembled in the lounge for liquid refreshments and comradely intercourse.

Stagner left the muted officers, and while driving to his family quarters on Avery Drive mulled mentally over the Department of Defense 's definition of treason, *"violation of the allegiance owed to ones sovereign or state and/or betrayal of ones Country"*. Upon arrival in his family quarters, he found the same definition in Webster unabridged dictionary and proceeded to the definition of sovereign which included, "having supreme rank, or authority", *"in the United States, this is the President of the United States"*.

Looking up on the wall to his framed presidential appointment to Captain in the regular Army of the United States, he read, "* and this officer is to observe and follow such orders and directions, from time to time, as may be given by me, or the future President of the United States Of America, or other Superior Officers acting in accordance with the laws of the United States of America". Stagner pondered. *"Col Dozier being the prime mover of the resolution was not realistic because Fort McClellan was commanded by a superior ranking combat arms officer. Col Dozier also exhibited a character and demeanor inconsistent with opposing the President of the United States"*. Stagner then reviewed his officer's oath of office and discovered the oath did not include obedience to the President of the United States whereas the oath of enlistment required obedience, *"the sojourner oath needs obedience to the president and allegiance to the Constitution"*.**

His neighbor, Major Amos Johnson was given a ride the next morning to his office in the 100th Chemical Group. Enroute, Stagner asked," What are you people trying to do?"

The Major replied, "Save this country from where it is going."

Stagner responded, "Where is it going?"

Major Amos Johnson did not reply. Arriving at destination, Johnson disembarked without comment.

Fort McClelland, located near Anniston, Alabama, on the route connecting Atlanta, Georgia, and Birmingham, Alabama, is in an area of the South seething with anger. The previous month, President Kennedy sent thirty thousand national guard troops to "Ole Miss". Two died and three hundred were wounded at the university in the successful racial integration of the University of Mississippi. Troops from Fort McClellan participated in the action. Attempts, by sympathetic Southerners, to register negroes for voting in Alabama were a constant source of friction among citizens. The newspapers were full of the Cuban missile crises: President Kennedy issued an Official Use Only Executive Order forbidding members of the military from discussing the word, "missile". For 1962 ,as of Oct., a total of 205 military lives were lost in Viet Nam and the number was increasing with each successive each month. President Kennedy had strong congressional and military opposition to the partial, aboveground, nuclear testing ban treaty being negotiated with Russia. Within the United States Army, a battle among the brass was being waged over the employment of "green beret" forces vis-à-vis conventional ground units. Military brass advocating the invasion of Cuba were backed by a U.S. Congressional Resolution if American interests were threatened , *"another example of expressed intent for decisive action without explicit definition of purpose"*.

Several weeks later ,while on duty as an instructor in the U. S. Army Chemical

School, Stagner was summoned to the school' s conference room. Upon entering he observed the seated presence of Col. La Verne Parks, Commandant of the school; Col. Wallace, Commanding Officer of the fort 's Noble Army Hospital; and Maj. Amos Johnson. Col. Parks ordered Stagner to take a seat at the conference table, handed him a pen and a sheet of paper and ordered him to make any changes desired. Stagner looked at the paper entitled ,"Resolution", *"this is not the resolution presented to the John C Calhoun Chapter # 343 of the National Sojourners and to which he expressed opposition"*. Stagner scanned the paper, handed it to the Col Parks without change or comment, saluted, and left the conference room, *"there now existed three witnesses to his acceptance of a Sojourner' s resolution without change after being given the opportunity to do. It was a military career death chamber".*

In early December,1962, Stagner attended a Sojourners, with wives, evening meeting at the Officers Club in which several new members took the oath of a Sojourner to protect and defend the United States of America against all enemies, domestic, or foreign, whomsoever. In attendance was Col. John Palmer, in civilian dress, recently retired from the U.S. Army as Commanding Officer of the Pine Bluff Arsenal in Arkansas where biological munitions were assembled. After the business part of the meeting, the slender Col. Palmer, singling out Stagner, in a low voice said, "The resolution also was also sent to the Pine Bluff Arsenal Sojourner Chapter(#166) where it was tabled by parliamentary procedure and so remains".

Stagner, *"an unaccountable killing of the resolution"*, responded, "Then you are aware of the local reading".

" My position as a local bank vice president involves community involvement. The Alabama Civil Air Patrol is interested in aerial radiological survey training. Will be in touch soon," countered Col. Palmer as he moved on-"

Immediately leaving the meeting Stagner thought, *"the resolution instigation did not originate with Col. Dozier. The resolution was dispatched from National Sojourners, Inc, Alexandria, Va. Distribution to two Sojourners Chapters means, by logical deduction, distribution to all National Sojourners Chapters located in military forts, bases ,and locations. He resolved never to attend another Sojourners meeting until the Sojourner 's oath included allegiance to the Constitution and Sojourner protocol eliminated the worst case scenario of a possible military coup de' etat.*

Capt. Stagner was redlined from promotion to the rank of Major in the Regular Army and offered, an enlistment with the rank of Sergeant. This was a possible means of achieving retirement from his present 1963 seventeen years of military service with the U.S. Army including two wars. Stagner declined the enlistment offer.

In the early spring of 1963, one of Stagner 's three daughters asked him to get her baptized. He and his older children were frequent Sunday morning attendees at the nondenominational church services conducted by an Army Chaplain in Fort McClellan 's nondenominational chapel . Stagner requested the chaplain, a major, to baptize his daughter.

The Chaplain asked, "To what denomination does she belong?"

"She does not belong to any church or denomination ," Stagner stipulated.

"She must belong to a church to be baptized," specified the Baptist Chaplain.
"This is a nondenominational chapel on a United States military fort and my daughter shall be baptized," Stagner adamantly countered. After considerable verbal intercourse among the fort `s administrative staff, the Chaplain, and an unyielding father, the baptism was scheduled on a Sunday morning in the post chapel. A large group of people were in attendance for the total immersion baptism of Stagner `s daughter.

A month later, upon his return from a day of instructing soldiers in radiological monitoring , Stagner `s wife greeted him with, "Our daughter was abused by our neighbor, Major Amos Johnson."

"When?"-,"*a brother Mason*".

"Today"

Stagner then advised his wife to immediately take their daughter to the fort `s military police headquarters and file an official complaint, "*should he file the complaint and interrogative stress applied to his wife or daughter result in change of story, courts martial charges could be filed against him for false accusations*". Stagner `s wife refused to file an official complaint.

Early in August,1963, an army sedan pulled up in front of Stagner `s family quarters on Avery Drive. A Lt. Col. stepped from the vehicle, walked with a military policeman up the steps, and rang the doorbell. Stagner, opening the door, received the command, "Get your gear together. You have thirty minutes before we leave". "*does the U.S. have gulags, remembering the bachelor Captain in the Germany Occupation who agreed with the Infantry in opposition to his Transportation superiors-his next assignment was Alaska*". Back at the door with his bag, he was met with, "Come with us". After entering the sedan, the Lt. Col. addressed Stagner,
"As of now your family quarters on Fort McClellan are off limits to you. You are being taken to the Bachelor Officers quarters for a room. Your station wagon will be delivered to you later today", "*what is going on? What is this about? Where are my children?*"

The next day ,a letter was received from a Calhoun County civil court judge which contained an order barring him from his family quarters on Fort McClellan, "*a civil county judge ordering a military person from his quarters on federal property was un heard of* ". His wife had filed for divorce, obtained custody of his five children, and had him evicted from his family quarters with a restraining order. Since the Commanding Officer of Fort McClellan promulgated the civil order, Stagner went to the post Judge Advocate for clarification. He was dismissed with, "An unwritten opinion supporting this action has been received from the Judge Advocate of the United States Army, "*the pentagon was involved*". Stagner obtained the services of an Anniston attorney to represent him in the divorce case, " *without an opportunity to defend himself ,he was being controlled equivalent to punishment*".

In late August, 1963, Stagner received, from Col. Laverne Parks, an order to report to the Mental Hygiene Clinic at the Noble Army Hospital at 1230 hours on 23 Aug.,1963 and as further directed. Reporting to the hospital, Stagner refused to talk

to the psychiatrist and was taken to the Col. Hull, Commanding Officer of the Hospital who sternly addressed Stagner,

"Captain Stagner, commit yourself for psychiatric treatment or you will be committed."

Stagner countered with, "You can try „Sir", saluted, did an about face, and left the office and hospital, "*this is remindful of something read concerning Russian political control*".

The next day, Stagner wrote Senator Dirksen concerning the events of the previous day and the order precipitating the events. On 19 September, 1963, the U.S. Army responded to Senator Dirksen`s inquiry on Stagner `s behalf. Col. Parks justified his order for sending Stagner to the mental hygiene clinic as, "for his own benefit in view of marital difficulties", "*what were the benefits Col. Parks had in mind*". Stagner also called the FBI in Birmingham which indicated no interest. He also wrote Drew Pearson who did not respond.

In a letter, dated 16, Oct., 1963, Capt. Stagner was again ordered by Col. Lavern Parks to report to the Commanding Officer, Noble Army Hospital and be admitted to the hospital within 24 hours because he would not submit to psychiatric interview. Upon reporting Stagner was restricted to the confines of the hospital where he must remain or be subject to courts martial for disobedience of a lawful order. He received multiple medical tests and treatment for painful joints. During his confinement to the hospital, the army doctors, nurses, and technicians made his confinement as pleasant and enjoyable as was within their means.

Sometime in early November, 1963, Stagner was advised that he would be evacuated by air to the Valley Forge General Hospital for further evaluation and treatment, "*the Sojourner resolution remained within him*". On the designated day, a passive tranquillized Capt. stood outside in uniform, with a large identification tag hanging from around his neck. A tin toy soldier waiting to be picked up.

Oaths of Enlistment and Oaths of Office

The wordings of the current oath of enlistment and oath for commissioned officers are as follows:

> "I, _____, do solemnly swear (or affirm) that I will support and defend the Constitution of the United States against all enemies, foreign and domestic; that I will bear true faith and allegiance to the same; and that I will obey the orders of the President of the United States and the orders of the officers appointed over me, according to regulations and the Uniform Code of Military Justice. So help me God." (Title 10, US Code; Act of 5 May 1960 replacing the wording first adopted in 1789, with amendment effective 5 October 1962).

> "I, _____ (SSAN), having been appointed an officer in the Army of the United States, as indicated above in the grade of _____ do solemnly swear (or affirm) that I will support and defend the Constitution of the United States against all enemies, foreign or domestic, that I will bear true faith and allegiance to the same; that I take this obligation freely, without any mental reservations or purpose of evasion; and that I will well and faithfully discharge the duties of the office upon which I am about to enter; So help me God." (DA Form 71, 1 August 1959, for officers.)

UNITED STATES ARMY CHEMICAL SCHOOL

OFFICE OF THE COMMANDANT

FORT McCLELLAN, ALABAMA

AJMCL-C

22 August 1963

SUBJECT: Medical Appointment

TO:

Captain Clyde H. Stagner
Military Art Division
U. S. Army Chemical School
Fort McClellan, Alabama

1. You are hereby directed to report to the Mental Hygiene Clinic, Noble Army Hospital, Fort McClellan, Alabama, at 1230 hours 23 August 1963.

2. You are to report again to the Mental Hygiene Clinic at 0730 hours on 28 August 1963 and at such other times as competent medical personnel of the Noble Army Hospital so direct.

L. A. Parks

L. A. PARKS
Colonel, CmlC
Commandant

THE COMMERCIAL NATIONAL BANK OF ANNISTON

ANNISTON, ALABAMA

JOHN M. PALMER
EXECUTIVE ASSISTANT
TO THE PRESIDENT

7 Jan 63

Dear Capt Stagner:

Check for 3.75 is to reimburse you for refreshments on the 29th. Thanks.

We enjoyed the hospitality and I have had many favorable comments on your conduct of the course.

If I can be of assistance to you some time, please let me know.

If our Bank would be useful, also, please advise.

Sincerely

JM Palmer

MEDICAL CONDITION – PHYSICAL PROFILE RECORD
(AR 40-501)

DATE: 7 August 1963

TO: Commanding Officer
U. S. Army Chemical Center & School
ATTN: Personnel Officer
Fort McClellan, Alabama

FROM: Commanding Officer
Noble Army Hospital
Fort McClellan, Alabama

LAST NAME - FIRST NAME - MIDDLE INITIAL, GRADE, SERVICE NO. AND ORGANIZATION

Stagner, Clyde Hurchel
Captain RA 0 65 183
USA Cml Sch

INSTRUCTIONS

Complete Section D of this form in lieu of DA Form 8-118 whenever a medical board is held for the sole purpose of permanently revising the physical profile to or from a numerical designator "3".

PREPARE COPIES AS INDICATED BELOW:
Unit Commander - 1 copy when Item 1 or 2 is checked
Appropriate Commander or HQ - 1 copy when Item 3 is checked.
Health Record Jacket, (DD Form 722) - 1 copy
Clinical Record - 1 copy when appropriate

SECTION A - DUTY STATUS *(Check Applicable Item(s))*

1	X	INDIVIDUAL IS RETURNED TO YOUR UNIT FOR DUTY *(AR 40-212, AR 635-40B, as applicable)*
2		INDIVIDUAL IS RETURNED TO YOUR UNIT FOR SEPARATION PROCESSING *(AR 40-212, AR 635-40B, as applicable)*
3	X	INDIVIDUAL (IS) (IS NOT) MEDICALLY QUALIFIED FOR duty AS EVIDENCED BY A MEDICAL EXAMINATION AND A REVIEW OF HIS HEALTH RECORD THIS DATE 25 July 63

SECTION B - PHYSICAL PROFILE
(Complete all items. When applicable "R" or "T" will be entered with numerical designator under appropriate factor)

		P	U	L	H	E	S	
4	PREVIOUS	1	1	1	1	1	1	PREVIOUS
5	PRESENT	1	1	1	1	1	1	PRESENT

6 INDIVIDUAL HAS THE DEFECT(S) LISTED BELOW. *(All defects requiring a 3 or 4 in any PULHES factor will be reported in non-technical language)*

☐ Continued under remarks

SECTION C - ASSIGNMENT RESTRICTIONS, OR GEOGRAPHICAL, OR CLIMATIC AREA LIMITATIONS *(Check Applicable Items(s))*

7	X	INDIVIDUAL REQUIRES NO MAJOR ASSIGNMENT, GEOGRAPHICAL, OR CLIMATIC AREA LIMITATIONS
8		MAJOR ASSIGNMENT, GEOGRAPHICAL, OR CLIMATIC AREA LIMITATIONS ARE ESTABLISHED BELOW *(AR 40-212, AR 40-501, AR 635-40B, as applicable. Describe specific assignment limitations or restrictions as outlined in Chapter 9, AR 40-501.)*

☐ Continued under remarks

9	X	THE ABOVE CONDITIONS ARE PERMANENT
10		THE ABOVE CONDITIONS ARE TEMPORARY. INDIVIDUAL IS TO REPORT TO A MEDICAL FACILITY ON *(Date)* ____ FOR FURTHER PHYSICAL PROFILE EVALUATION OR MEDICAL TREATMENT AND DISPOSITION *(AR 40-212, AR 40-501 as applicable)*
11		SEPARATION OR RETIREMENT OF THIS INDIVIDUAL WILL NOT BE EFFECTED WITHOUT PRIOR MEDICAL EVALUATION *(AR 40-212, AR 40-501, AR 616-41, as applicable)*
12	X	THIS SUPERSEDES PREVIOUS MEDICAL CONDITION - PHYSICAL PROFILE RECORDS

13. TYPED NAME & GRADE OF AUTHORIZED OFFICER AT MEDICAL FACILITY: WILLIAM P. ARGY, CAPT., MC

SIGNATURE: [signature]

DA FORM 1 FEB 62 8-274

NOBLE ARMY HOSPITAL
FORT McCLELLAN, ALABAMA

AJMMD-O 14 October 1963

Memorandum for Record. Re: Capt Clyde Stagner.

1. Captain Stagner came to my office voluntarily, when he heard that I had been trying to reach him, at approximately 1000 hours 14 October 1963.

2. Captain Stagner was informed that the Medical Board held for him on Friday, 11 October 1963, had been returned for reconsideration and that any further action by the Board and re-submission to the Commanding Officer, Noble Army Hospital, must be accompanied by a psychiatric interview.

3. Captain Stagner was pleasant and most cooperative. After much statement with regards to the accompanying problems of his case, he was reminded of the extremely limited area in which the Board could function. He stated that he would not consider a psychiatric interview until after the divorce proceedings with his wife were completed in about two weeks. He would make a decision then as to whether he would accept a psychiatric interview. He stated that he desired Capt. Sarner to be aware of the "environment of his case" and that he wished for his lawyer to present certain elements of his case to the psychiatrist. I questioned him again as to whether he would submit to a psychiatric interview and he reiterated that he would not until after the divorce proceedings.

4. I questioned him as to whether this should be his official answer to the Board and he stated that it should. Captain Stagner also stated that he wished to remove his statement regarding the prejudice of Colonel Lull in the case. He stated also that if admitted to this installation and transferred to any hospital that it would be "under duress" and that he would give no information to anybody under these circumstances. Finally, Captain Stagner requested a copy of all proceedings of this Board to date.

William P. Argo
WILLIAM P. ARGO
Captain, MC

DEPARTMENT OF THE ARMY
OFFICE OF THE SECRETARY OF THE ARMY
WASHINGTON 25, D.C.

19 September 1963

Honorable Everett McKinley Dirksen

United States Senate

Dear Senator Dirksen:

This letter is in reply to your further inquiry in behalf of Captain Clyde H. Stagner, 065183.

Captain Stagner was referred to the mental hygiene clinic at Fort McClellan, Alabama, by his commanding officer, for his own benefit in view of recent marital difficulties. Captain Stagner did not submit a formal request for the presence of legal counsel during the clinical appointment. He did discuss the possibility of obtaining legal counsel with a judge advocate officer. Since the referral was not for any disciplinary or adverse administrative purpose, the Staff Judge Advocate saw no reason for Captain Stagner to be represented by legal counsel; however, he was advised by counsel that he was not required to make any statements to the examining psychiatrist.

Captain Stagner did not voluntarily cooperate with the psychiatrist during the interviews. He declined to make any statements whatsoever, citing his rights under Article 31, Uniform Code of Military Justice. Since adverse personnel action is not involved in this case, additional interviews in the mental hygiene clinic are not anticipated.

Your continued interest in this matter is appreciated.

Sincerely,

Inclosure

G. W. PICKELL
Lt Colonel, GS
Office, Chief of
Legislative Liaison

Incl #3

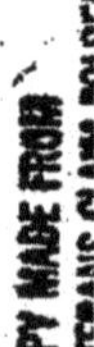

NOBLE ARMY HOSPITAL
FORT McCLELLAN, ALABAMA

AJMHD-O

14 October 1963

Memorandum for Record. Re: Capt Clyde Stagner.

1. Captain Stagner came to my office voluntarily, when he heard that I had been trying to reach him, at approximately 1000 hours 14 October 1963.

2. Captain Stagner was informed that the Medical Board held for him on Friday, 11 October 1963, had been returned for reconsideration and that any further action by the Board and re-submission to the Commanding Officer, Noble Army Hospital, must be accompanied by a psychiatric interview.

3. Captain Stagner was pleasant and most cooperative. After much statement with regards to the accompanying problems of his case, he was reminded of the extremely limited area in which the Board could function. He stated that he would not consider a psychiatric interview until after the divorce proceedings with his wife were completed in about two weeks. He would make a decision then as to whether he would accept a psychiatric interview. He stated that he desired Capt. Sarner to be aware of the "environment of his case" and that he wished for his lawyer to present certain elements of his case to the psychiatrist. I questioned him again as to whether he would submit to a psychiatric interview and he reiterated that he would not until after the divorce proceedings.

4. I questioned him as to whether this should be his official answer to the Board and he stated that it should. Captain Stagner also stated that he wished to remove his statement regarding the prejudice of Colonel Lull in the case. He stated also that if admitted to this installation and transferred to any hospital that it would be "under duress" and that he would give no information to anybody under these circumstances. Finally, Captain Stagner requested a copy of all proceedings of this Board to date.

William P. Argy

WILLIAM P. ARGY
Captain, MC

Stagner

UNITED STATES ARMY CHEMICAL SCHOOL
FORT McCLELLAN, ALABAMA

Office of the
COMMANDANT

AJMCL-C

16 October 1963

SUBJECT: Medical Appointment

TO: Captain Clyde H. Stagner
Military Art Division
U. S. Army Chemical School
Fort McClellan, Alabama

1. I have been advised by the Commanding Officer, Noble Army Hospital, that you have refused to submit to psychiatric interview and that it is necessary that you be evaluated by a Psychiatrist in order that a Medical Board action pending can be completed.

2. You are directed to report within 24 hours of receipt of this letter to the Commanding Officer, Noble Army Hospital, Fort McClellan, Alabama, for admission in order to complete the proceedings of your Medical Board.

L. A. Parks
L. A. PARKS
Colonel, CmlC
Commandant

Will write you when I end up wherever they assign me

Clyde

To all who shall see these presents, greeting:

Know Ye, that reposing special trust and confidence in the patriotism, valor, fidelity and abilities of Clyde Hurchel Stagner, *I do appoint him* Second Lieutenant, Transportation Corps *in the*

Army of the United States

such appointment to date from the second *day of* February *nineteen hundred and* forty-nine. *He is therefore carefully and diligently to discharge the duty of the office to which he is appointed by doing and performing all manner of things thereunto belonging.*

He will enter upon active duty under this commission only when specifically ordered to such active duty by competent authority.

And I do strictly charge and require all Officers and Soldiers under his command when he shall be employed on active duty, to be obedient to his orders as an officer of his grade and position. And he is to observe and follow such orders and directions, from time to time, as he shall receive, from me, or the future President of the United States of America, or the General or other Superior Officers set over him, according to the rules and discipline of War.

This Commission evidences an appointment in the Army of the United States under the provisions of section 37, National Defense Act, as amended, and is to continue in force for a period of five years from the date above specified, and during the pleasure of the President of the United States, for the time being.

Done at the City of Washington, this fifteenth *day of* March *in the year of our Lord, one thousand nine hundred and* forty-nine, *and of the Independence of the United States of America the one hundred and* seventy-third.

By the President:

UNITED STATES OF AMERICA WAR OFFICE

Edward F. Witsell
Major General
The Adjutant General.

To all who shall see these presents, greeting:

Know Ye, that reposing special trust and confidence in the patriotism, valor, fidelity and abilities of Clyde Lurchel Stagner *, I do appoint* him Captain, Regular Army *in the*

Army of the United States

to rank *as such from the* twenty-sixth *day of* February *, nineteen hundred and* fifty-six *. This Officer will therefore carefully and diligently discharge the duties of the office to which appointed by doing and performing all manner of things thereunto belonging.*

And I do strictly charge and require those Officers and other personnel of lesser rank to render such obedience as is due an officer of this grade and position. And this Officer is to observe and follow such orders and directions, from time to time, as may be given by me, or the future President of the United States of America, or other Superior Officers acting in accordance with the laws of the United States of America.

This commission is to continue in force during the pleasure of the President of the United States of America, for the time being, under the provisions of those Public Laws relating to Officers of the Armed Forces of the United States of America *and the component thereof in which this appointment is made.*

Done at the City of Washington, this sixteenth *day of* November, *in the year of our Lord one thousand nine hundred and* fifty-six *, and of the Independence of the United States of America the one hundred and* eighty-first.

By the President:

John A. Klein
Major General
The Adjutant General

Wilber M. Brucker.
Secretary of the Army

DD FORM 1 OCT 49 1A REPLACES NME FORM 1A, 1 SEP 48, WHICH MAY BE USED.

CHAPTER 2

WINTER at VALLEY FORGE

Arriving at the airfield, what appeared to be two engine C46 aircraft, painted white with a large red cross on its side, stood alone with boarding stairs dropped to the ground., *"this is like the olive drab aircraft traveled in along the New Guinea coastline from Buna to Biak in 1944".* Stagner was escorted, assisted aboard, and seated in the front row. As the engines revved up, he was administered a pill by a perpetually smiling Air Force nurse. Moving among other patients, she cooed and clucked forth readily available smiles from faint to framed teeth.

Floating upward, Stagner was in a slow motion time capsule going from somewhere to an unknown nowhere. There was no conversation. The patient passengers were neatly egg crated and buckled, *"everything was smooth"*. There was no movement, *"were my children alright, of course my children were alright"*. The airplane sang a song of h`m, h`m, h`m, h`m followed by h`m, h`m , h`m. In what seemed like a short spasm of time, the beautiful nurse announced our arrival in Montgomery, Alabama where we would be billeted for the night.

Arrival at the billets included a pill with a small paper cup of water overviewed by a good looking nurse who ascertained the consumption thereof. Some pleasant tasting food followed after which a plain room containing a cot was assigned. Pill sleep came immediately, *"how were my childr --"*. Next morning, the pill procedure was repeated before leaving the billets. Up-up and away was repeated on several intermediate stops before the engines were silenced at the Fort Dix, New Jersey, airfield late in the afternoon, *"the place has changed since serving here in the 9th Infantry division in 1951"*.

After some food in an army mess hall, Stagner and two other patients were escorted into a drab army bus which was jerked into motion before heading into the sunset, *"no pill this trip, what is happening"*. With every few miles, Stagner `s senses sharpened. The bus driver `s silhouette outline became clearly outlined against the headlights playing ahead on the hilly curves. No conversation; only noisy monotonous engine collaboration Several hours later, the bus passed through a gate displaying "Valley Forge General Hospital".

Stopping in front of a door marked entrance, Stagner was met and escorted into a receiving room. A Sergeant ordered the Captain to remove his clothes, *"patients in hospitals have no rank"*. That done, came the order to put on a pair of pajamas made to fit a soldier twice Stagner `s size. Then a plastic patient identification band was placed around a wrist. That done, came the order to remove the gold band ring on his right hand ring finger which displayed the Jewish letter Yod centered in a black triangle, *"until death do us part is engraved inside the ring band"*.

"No!" resounded Stagner who continued wearing the ring.

A Captain of the hospital staff entered and briefly interviewed Stagner, *"he has no knowledge of why I am here"*. A calendar an the wall read, "October 28.1963",*"what will it read on the way out"*.

A male medic, dressed in white, entered from an inside door and courteously

directed Stagner to accompany him. After twenty minutes of following covered corridor after covered corridor connecting different buildings, the medic unlocked a door for their entrance. Inside was another medic who silently verified Stagner `s ID bracelet, unlocked an inner door with a small security screened window, ordered Stagner inside a dark abyss and then locked the door behind him.

A wall light flickered on out lining humans on cots, some weaving up and down. In the dimness, the sources of the wailing, sobbing, and "I am the Savoir" were blended without harmony. Suffering humanity awakened Stagner frequently from his light, fitful sleep, "*is this immersion in human fragility by design , an attempt to lower self esteem below the bare ribs of reason. cleaning sewer lines to support my family was long ago accepted*". Morning finally arrived with his name called. After breakfast, he was interviewed by two doctors in sequence. Sometime later, he accompanied the white clad medic through several covered connecting building corredors. The medic stopped at another metal door with screen covered small window and rang a buzzer. Stagner thought, "*was this a secured ward for unfortunate military folk*".

A buzzer sounded allowing the opening of the door for Stagner `s entrance into a closed, meaning confinement, ward. After being assigned a cot, he explored the facility. Three quarters of the ward contained cots. At one end, towards the entrance door, was the nurse `s screen protected cage: across the hall were doctor` s offices At the other end was a leisure room, with seating, containing books, magazines, and a television. On one side was a patio, as long as the ward, which looked down on the thick interwoven wire mesh capable of preventing escape . The patients were all male.

"Breakfast," sounded the orderly. Patients formed a single line.

"No talking," admonished the orderly as the door was opened and the pajama clad some things moved as a winding snake from the closed ward to the mess hall on the floor below. Issued, one at a time, was a metal tray, a dull knife, fork , and spoon. The line then snaked its way along a line of cafeteria type servers followed by orderly seating at picnic type tables.

At a given time after the last patient was served , the orderly sounded off,

"No talking".

The patients rose, formed into their line, turned in their utensils under the watchful eye of an inspecting kitchen accountant, and slowly shuffled out of the mess hall. After administering supervised swallowing of medications back in the closed ward, relaxation, or time killing, occurred until, at 10AM, the nurse announced, "Doctor `s rounds". Patients stood at the foot of their cots as the psychiatrist toured the ward with a nurse and orderly. Questions were asked, comments were made. Patients said little, if anything. Coming to Stagner, the psychiatrist, owl eyed Dr. Fisher, stopped, looked at him and, without comment, proceeded to the next patient, "*why am I here*". As of 10 AM, Stagner had yet to be medicated.

Lunch procedure was a replica of breakfast. Following lunch, Stagner `s roaming around the ward confines included conversation exchanges with patients. A tall,

bald patient identified himself as a reserve colonel from Fort Wadsworth located across the narrows from Brooklyn, New York, *"lived in Brooklyn across the narrows when my daughter, Nicki, was born in a naval hospital on Long Island".* Another was a medium height , introverted patient who reluctantly identified himself as a Lt. Col. Army chaplain. There was a Maj. evacuated from Korea, several Sergeants, with the remainder being privates. Remarkably, all the patients were friendly with respect shown to all other patients and without any rancor to superior rank. Only one patient, an exception, lay continually curled up in the fetal position on his cot. Stagner noticed a male nurse of medium height, slender, in his thirties, with short wavy hair, present and observing him at a distance.

Late in the afternoon, Stagner approached the nurse `s cage and, in response to a female `s, "Can I Help you?"

Stagner asked, "why am I here?"

" You know why you are here," the nurse responded.

"I do not know why I am here and I want to know why I am here." Stagner iterated. The nurse went to her telephone for a muted conversation after which Stagner was told, "the Chief of the Psychiatric Department will be here in a few minutes to talk to you."

Stagner looked at the ward clock, the only time measurement available in the closed ward, *"what day is this in November".* Ten minutes later, the ward door opened allowing a paunchy Lt. Col., wearing the medical caduceus on his uniform lapels, to enter.

"Are you Stagner", he demanded.

"Yes Sir, why am I here?" asked Stagner.

"You know why you are here." admonished the Lt. Col..

"Why am I here?" demanded Stagner.

"You are in a lot of trouble!" came the clipped response.

"What trouble am I in?" persevered Stagner as the patients gathered.

"You know what trouble you` re in," snipped the agitated Lt. Col. As he turned and exited the ward.

The patients lined up for the evening meal and were listening; but not looking.

The following morning after breakfast and doctor `s rounds, Stagner was summoned into Dr. Fischer `s office across from the nurse `s cage. Entering, the doctor motioned to a chair facing the desk and the doctor. Nothing was said. The silence ensued for lengthy minutes as the two eye measured each other. Finally, Dr Fisher sternly quipped, "you can go". As Stagner left, " *is he going to educate me or am I going to educate him".* Outside the door, the Col. ,escorted by an orderly, passed by in a dazed look with a reddish, quarter sized abrasion on his temple. Stagner sought out the chaplain for an explanation.

"Red spots on the temple are the residual results of electric shock. He will be looking somewhere from nowhere until tomorrow when he will slowly come back with us minus some memory," explained the chaplain.

"How is the need for it determined?" asked Stagner in high awareness.

"If the doctor recommends shock treatment the recommendation can be

implemented by the patient `s volunteer agreement, or, if the patient is declared incompetent, the recommendation can be implemented by the spouses approval. Beyond that requires a court decision", the chaplain added, "unless the this hospital declares him incompetent and transfers him directly to a Veterans Administration Hospital and an unknown fate." Stagner thanked the chaplain, "*my wife filed for divorce-she will happily give her approval to my shock treatment- is this visit for memory erasing*".

The male nurse was watching.

Shortly after lunch, the orderly announce, "Patients meeting".

The patients gathered in the center of the ward between the row of cots. A patient, who was a Sergeant, stated the purpose of the meeting, "Patient Smith says he is ready for open ward. You a can vote yes by raising your right hands." The number of hands raised was less than the total patients present. Patient Smith remained on the closed ward. The chaplain, standing next to Stagner elaborated, "Patient `s vote for open ward is the first step on getting out of here. The second step is getting the psychiatrist to agree with the patients. No patient is going to get out of here, regardless of how the patients vote, unless the psychiatrist wants them to leave. it's a manipulative game."

The Sergeant, conducting the meeting, declared, "I nominate Capt. Stagner to be our patient representative". The yes vote was unanimous. Stagner could not refuse, "*having commanded an Infantry Company and an Armored Personnel Carrier Company, my best effort might help these men*".

At doctor `s rounds on day three, Dr. Fisher advised Stagner that a tranquilizer was prescribed for him, " *relaxation to verbal expression*". After the rounds, the names of 12 patients were called including Stagner `s. Formed into a line ,an orderly escorted them from the ward to an adjacent open conference room with chairs formed in a circle. After random seating, Dr. Fisher joined the group in his reserved seat.

"For the new patients this is group therapy, feel free to join in the discussions at any time unless told otherwise," explicated Dr. Fisher who added, "Jones, what concerns you the most this morning?".

"Who is screwing my sheep while I`m gone," Jones seriously replied.

The session went on for twenty minutes listening to the depravations of sexual deviants with sisters , mothers, and animals, "*or so they want Fisher to believe*". Sex with animals was the most prolific for the vociferous. Several patients remained reticent or answered Dr. Fisher `s questions with a yes or no. When asked his question, Stagner shrugged his shoulders, "*he needs volitional conflicting patient expression to do his job.*" Other than the sexual dissertations, the participating patients commented, or criticized, each other with considerable self control, "*he may disagree with you but he is your buddy*". An hour later, Dr. Fisher rose and left the group, "*how can Fisher remember what conversations transpired without a tape recorder in his pocket or a bug on the room*".

Returning from lunch, the patients were divided into the Work Therapy Groups which were escorted to their various locations. Stagner chose wood working

and started making a chess board, *"this place reminds me of a big chess board".* Some patients chatted freely with others; others were stoic and remote. Several orderlies monitored all patient using tools. The environment was conducive to relaxation without stress. The male nurse, a silent sentry, was there observing.

A couple of evenings later ,the nurse in the cage informed Stagner at the head of the pill taking line, " Dr. Fisher has put you on stelazine , *"nice to know the future hellos will come to a dimmed brain rather than cognizant one".*

The following days were repetitive. Stagner called a patient meeting when requested and always voted the patient` s release to the psychiatric open ward of the Psychiatric Department. The chaplain, major, several sergeants ,and enlisted men left the closed ward. The colonel and other patients periodically returned from somewhere with bright red spots on their temples. Stagner` s short duration office visits with Dr. Fisher included trivia conversation without reference to his military or personal life. On November 18, Stagner was transferred to the open ward of the Psychiatric Department.

Sitting in the end room after lunch one day, Stagner was scanning a Reader` s Digest between glances at the television screen. Normal programming was interrupted by Walter Cronkite emotionally declaring, "The President has been shot". Patients filled the room. Afternoon patient activities centered around the television screen. Stagner could no longer discern the words in the Reader `s Digest: he could not concentrate. He saw the male nurse on the other side of the room, *"to hell with him".* Although he wanted to cry, only tears were rolling rolled down his cheeks, *"were the sojourners involved, could so many good, patriotic Sojourners be manipulated into treason by a few ranking 'vested interest' Sojourners".* As the terrible tragedy unfolded throughout the entire afternoon: the ward became a tomb.

Although Stagner was in physical pain, he went to a screened window and concentrated on the white steeple sitting in the valley several miles away, *"and God".* An orderly interrupted him back to reality with some medication. Although among soldiers, he was terribly alone. The worst case scenario had arrived, *"time for the controlled fear mode. plan for the worst case, count your benefits if results are otherwise. plan multiple responses allowing selection of choice. Anticipate worst actions from integral players permitting viable responses. It was Friday, November 22, held inside military walls since Oct.,16".*

Stagner had dispatched a letter to a lawyer friend on November 8th with the orderly` s comment that all mail, in and out, was censored. A week later he had the name of Joseph Restifo, J.D, of Philadelphia, who was later hired and represented Stagner for the remainder of his mandated stay at the Valley Forge General Hospital.

Communication with Dr. Fisher became polite, courteous phrases accompanied by a the shades of a smile. Within a week, Stagner was sent to the psychiatric open ward where he was assigned a room with minimum furniture, *"perhaps residue from the 1770` s".* Patients wore pajamas but were allowed to eat in the appropriate hospital mess, i.e., officers ate in the officer` s mess. On weekends, if a pass was permitted after request, *"reward and punishment protocol",* uniforms were returned for week end visits to surrounding communities. An adjacent lot was

available for patients to park their automobiles during the week, "*mobility for monitored social intercourse* " . Patients remained under the purview of the Psychiatric Department.

On a morning soon after President Kennedy` s assassination, Stagner dispatched an uncensored letter to the Adjutant General, United States Army, Wash, D.C. in which he demanded his immediate release from the United States Army. The response came several nights later at midnight. A knock on his door awoke Stagner as two white clad orderlies barged in with the command,

"Outside, now!"

Outside the room, he was positioned between four orderlies who followed Capt. Dr. Fisher back to the closed ward whence Stagner came, "*thank heavens there was no goose step*". Back at the closed ward, Dr. Fisher snipped, "Your in closed ward until the patients vote your release." At 10 AM the next morning, the patients voted Stagner to open ward. Dr.Fisher then advised Stagner that he would have to wait until Monday, "*must ride this out without resentful emotion or the trip back to open ward may evaporate*". OnMonday, Stagner went back to the psychiatric open ward.

On December 9th, because of an adverse reaction, Dr. Fisher stopped the stelazine regimen and advised Stagner never to take the medication again, "*thank you, Dr. Fisher, your orders shall be followed to the letter*". On February 27,1964, Stagner was medically discharged from the Psychiatric Department and obtained a room in the hospital`s bachelor officer`s quarters referred to as the BOQ. These quarters were also occupied by members of the hospital staff. The second day of occupancy, Stagner was shaving in the BOQ latrine when the male nurse, "*the closed ward Hawkeye*", entered, started shaving, paused, looked at Stagner and quietly declared,

"You know you have lost you security clearance."

"Know it, now for sure" Stagner quipped back while continuing to shave.

" Have you any documents or drawings?" continued the nurse.

"None," responded Stagner, "*what would be done if he knew about all those in my Head, custom made electric shock*".

The nurse left the latrine leaving Stagner pondering, "*who is paying this nurse dwelling in something outside the scope of medical treatment. Is he army intelligence, FBI, CIA or some other unpublished acronym.* "

Over the next few weeks, Stagner investigated military dependant`s monetary claims for household appliance damaged in shipment from Germany to the United States. The evening meals in the hospital Officer`s Mess were followed by visitation to the small officer` s club lounge for television, comrade conversation, and a beer. While medical boards were being administratively processed with time consuming deliberation, Stagner floated day by day in a limbo wondering when the mental and physical controls would be completely removed. Finally, his lawyer advised that the hospital and U.S. Army Medical Boards, respectively, had recommended medical military retirement for paranoid personality, specific diagnosis of suspiciousness, with thirty per cent disability, "*this place got that right because I sure am suspicious*".

Based on the probability of medical retirement, Stagner planned the future based on the available information in an almanac. Fresno, California, had a good Standard of Living Index, a dry warm climate, and Fresno State University, "*a desirable environment for the children*". On May 1, 1964, Stagner was medically retired from the United States Army with eighteen years, and one day, service. Two weeks later, with a wife and five children in a Chevrolet station wagon, the journey to Fresno began.

The retirement included the subsequent receipt of an official packet containing a U. S. Army Manual delineating, for retired regular army officers, the restrictions concerning criticizing certain elected officials. Much of the manual content was an elaboration and explanation of the Articles contained in the U.S. Courts Martial Manual, all of which were applicable to retired U. S. Army Regular Officers. In addition to the manual, the packet contained official instructions ostracizing Captain Clyde H. Stagner, U.S. Army, Retired from social and/or industrial contact with members of the U.S. Military Forces. Upon reading the latter, Stagner thought, "*perhaps isolation to a leper colony is next on the agenda, is this money for silence with boundary conditions, are my children safe*".

SPECIAL ORDERS NUMBER 101	DATE 23 April 1964	HEADQUARTERS DEPARTMENT OF THE ARMY WASHINGTON 25, D. C. EXTRACT

CHECK | INSTRUCTIONS: INDICATE PARAGRAPH TO BE USED BY ENTERING AN "X" IN THE APPROPRIATE BOX

XX PARA 173. TC 440. CAPT CLYDE H STAUNER 065183 CMLC

having been determined to be perm unfit for dy by reason of phys disability of 30 percent incurred while entitled to rec basic pay is ret from active svc with gr and ret pay of Capt as prov by title 10, United States Code, secs 1201 and 1372. He is rel from asg XXXXX Med Holding Co Valley Forge Gen Hosp Phoenixville Pa EDCSA: 30 Apr 1964 placed on USA Ret List 1 May 1964

On ~~he is trf to USAR (Ret Res) and asgd to USAR Con Gp (Ret) USARCEN St Louis 32, Mo.~~

HOSTWOY. PCS. TDN. PPSIA. 2142010 01-1731-1732-1733-1735-1736-1737 P 1517 S99-999. SPN 563

PARA

having been determined to be unfit for dy by reason of phys disability of percent incurred while entitled to rec basic pay his name is placed upon the temp disability ret list of the Army with gr and ret pay of as prov by title 10, United States Code, secs 1202 and 1372. He is rel from asg and dy

On he is trf to USAR (Ret Res) and asgd to USAR Con Gp (Ret) USARCEN St Louis 32, Mo.

HOSTWOY. PCS. TDN. PPSIA. 2142010 01-1731-1732-1733-1735-1736-1737 P 1517 S99-999. SPN 562

By Order of the Secretary of the Army:

EARLE G. WHEELER,
General, United States Army,
Chief of Staff.

Official:

J. C. LAMBERT,
Major General, United States Army,
The Adjutant General.

DA FORM 330
OCT 62

PREVIOUS EDITIONS OF THIS FORM ARE OBSOLETE

855409

Incl #2

Standard Form 509
(Rev. August 1954)
Bureau of the Budget
Circular A-32

CLINICAL RECORD | **DOCTOR'S PROGRESS NOTES** (*Sign all notes*)

DATE

28 Oct 63 This is the case of a 39 year old WM Captain with approximately 17 years service who was transferred here from Fort McClellan, Ala. possibly due to "confused" state of affairs following patient's medical board. Patient is "under charges" and did not desire psychiatric hospitalization.

M.S. tonight reveals a well-oriented young appearing man with clear sensorium. Vehemently denies psychiatric disorder. Patient is verbal. no clear evidence of paranoid ideation

Imp: Psychiatric Observation

W. N. Boyleton, Capt MC

(Continue on reverse side)

PATIENT'S IDENTIFICATION (*For typed or written entries give: Name—last, first, middle; grade; date; hospital or medical facility*) | REGISTER NO. | WARD NO.

STAGNER CLYDE H CPT
6 750.5 2-22 193

VALLEY FORGE AH
260D

DOCTOR'S PROGRESS NOTES
Standard Form 509
509-106

KENNETH A. ROBERTS
AT LARGE, ALABAMA

DISTRICT OFFICE:
FEDERAL BUILDING
ANNISTON, ALABAMA

COMMITTEE:
INTERSTATE AND FOREIGN
COMMERCE

CHAIRMAN, SUBCOMMITTEE:
PUBLIC HEALTH AND SAFETY

Congress of the United States
House of Representatives
Washington, D. C.

October 24, 1963

Captain Clyde H. Stagner
Mil. Art. Div
USA Cml School
Fort McClellan, Alabama

Dear Captain Stagner:

Thank you for your recent letter regarding your hospitalization at Fort McClellan, Alabama.

I can certainly understand and sympathize with your situation and will be happy to contact the Department of the Army in your behalf. Just as soon as information can be received, I will further advise you.

With every good and kind wish, I am

Very sincerely,

Kenneth A. Roberts

Kenneth A. Roberts

KAR:wwg

GUY SPARKS
ATTORNEY AT LAW

409 COMMERCIAL NATIONAL BANK BLDG.
PHONE ADAMS 7-5711 ANNISTON, ALABAMA

October 25, 1963

Colonel George F. Lull, Jr.
Commanding Officer
Noble Army Hospital
Fort McClellan, Alabama

Dear Colonel Lull:

This will confirm our telephone conversation of this afternoon wherein you requested that I write this letter regarding Captain Clyde H. Stagner. You will recall that it was your opinion today that Captain Stagner should not presently be informed of the fact that the Circuit Court of this County will proceed to determine a support award for his children on October 29, 1963.

Briefly, the situation is this: Captain Stagner's wife filed suit for divorce against him, seeking alimony, custody of the four children, a property division, attorney's fees and a divorce. Captain Stagner desires to defeat the divorce and effect a reconciliation with his wife. The case was set to be tried on its merits on October 29, 1963. Captain Stagner has now been hospitalized and is being sent out of this State. He will not be available for the trial on October 29th.

The Circuit Court will not proceed with the divorce and alimony aspects of this case on October 29th. It will proceed to hear and determine the question of child support during the interim period pending final outcome of the case. This will involve a determination by the Court on October 29th of how much money Captain Stagner will be legally required to pay for the support of his children during this period.

From a legal point of view it is desirable for Captain Stagner to be advised of this fact, which is what I would have done today in the absence of your opinion of its possible effect on him. For him to be unavailable itself presents many legal difficulties. Not knowing his attitude, or wishes or instructions will make my legal responsibilities difficult to fulfill. It will also make a decision more difficult for the Court. From a purely legal point of view, Captain Stagner is entitled to know what is going on. He cannot otherwise act to attempt to carry out his wishes.

I would like to request that he be advised of this situation and that he be allowed to contact me in regard to it. I of course understand

Colonel George F. Lull, Jr.
October 25, 1963
Page Two

your decision today and I also understand your desire to consult further before making a final decision.

Thank you for your co-operation. If I can be of any further service in this or any other regard, I hope you will let me know.

Sincerely,

Guy Sparks
GUY SPARKS

GS/s
cc: Honorable William C. Bibb

NOBLE ARMY HOSPITAL
FORT McCLELLAN, ALABAMA

AJMMD-C 28 October 1963

SUBJECT: Captain Clyde H. Stagner

TO: Chief, Neuropsychiatric Service
Valley Forge General Hospital
Phoenixville, Penna.

1. The above-named patient was recently transferred to your facility for observation and disposition. He is scheduled for release from active duty on 31 December, this year, but has applied for earlier release.

2. His medical records indicate an emotional or psychiatric disorder extending over a number of years. His recent actions suggested to me that, whatever his difficulty, it was becoming worse. In the process of meeting a Medical Board, he was uncooperative and uncommunicative. In order to protect his rights, I indicated to Captain Stagner's commanding officer that he should be hospitalized for psychiatric evaluation to complete the board action.

3. At the time that Captain Stagner was ordered into the hospital, he was not only uncooperative and uncommunicative, but he was also disturbed, and he had exhibited some rather bizarre behavior that was proving to be a continuing problem to the command. To some degree, this was associated with a pending divorce action by his wife.

4. During his period of hospitalization, Captain Stagner quieted down considerably and became much more cooperative. On the afternoon prior to his scheduled evacuation, I received a call from Captain Stagner's attorney who wished to inform him of the planned action in the local court. It was my decision that, since Captain Stagner could not really do much to influence the action of the court, he should not be informed of this at that time. I felt that the information might result in a reversion of his behavior pattern and make his evacuation more difficult.

5. The inclosed letter from Captain Stagner's attorney is forwarded to you. The decision to pass this information on to Captain Stagner is left up to you.

AJMMD-C 28 October 1963
SUBJECT: Captain Clyde H. Stagner

6. I might add that the court was concerned that this medical evacuation was a ruse on the part of Captain Stagner, with the connivance of the Army, to remove himself from the court's jurisdiction. I pointed out that Captain Stagner would be returned here for duty and separation if no psychiatric disorder were found. I further noted that if, in fact, Captain Stagner was mentally ill, then the court would have to act under a different set of circumstances.

7. Although Captain Stagner cannot accept it, everything that has happened in connection with this hospitalization has been directed to a protection of his interests.

George F. Lull Jr.

1 Incl
as

GEORGE F. LULL, JR.
Colonel, MC
Commanding

2

Radiological Branch
U. S. Army Chemical School
Fort McClellan, Alabama
27 November 1963

Lt Colonel Tuttle
Chief, N&P Service
Valley Forge Hospital
Phoenixville, Pennsylvania

Dear Colonel Tuttle:

A short time ago I received a letter from Captain Clyde H. Stagner requesting that I write you regarding his hospitalization. He neglected, however, to inform me as to the exact nature this correspondence should take.

I have served with Captain Stagner for three years and worked in the same office with him. If you think I might have any information regarding Captain Stagner that may be helpful to you I would be more than happy to send it to you.

Sincerely yours,

Charles F. Lemr

CHARLES F. LEMR
Major, CmlC

Stagner, Chant

8 Nov 63

Dear Don,

Received your letter of the 6th this AM. The photostat enclosed was the one ordering me to this hospital. The copy I read is of the order in which Col Parker ordered me into Noble Army Hospital, Fort McClellan because I wouldn't talk to the psychiatrist.

Have been in this closed ward since 29 October under observation. I've never been on a submarine but from the rumors this is similar by analogy. Letters are censored going out and possibly coming in.

Dr Fischer will not permit me a ground pass to walk around the hospital grounds because I won't talk to him. Consequently I may be under this duress for some time to come since he (Dr Fischer) has a general reputation here of being a little "thick headed" but also a good psychiatrist and hard worker. Every day here strengthens my conviction (learned in the US Army) of remaining silent under duress such as this. I also hope my physical condition does not worsen because, in my opinion, it would constitute individual professional negligence on the part of Dr Fischer.

Regards to Mary Anne and I hope to hear from you soon.

Sincerely,

Clyde

DATE	1963 3	DATE	4
	Allergic to Novocain & Procaine - See records.		Bus Trip (Sightseeing c̄ other pts.) Pt remains @ same. Quiet - little to say - Smiles pleasantly.
2900	Pt trans to ward 26C. Capt Fisher SFC Butler		R Walker
	0930hrs. Received as trans from 26D		
	A&D office notified. (Spc Wheeler)	13 Nov	Appt. c̄ I.G. @ 1500 Concurrence c̄ Capt Fisher.
	[illegible]		
Nov	1400hrs Pt is friendly & co-operative. Spends quite a bit of time talking to pts. Pete. Does not discuss his problems freely c̄ staff. "I'll talk when I'm ready."	13 Nov	0910 thanked nurse for her "words of wisdom" ??? When asked about GI, yet was suggested he speak freely c̄ MO of his problems. [illegible]
	[illegible]		
9 Nov	1330-1500 - Allowed to go on		

DATE	5	DATE	Received on 27AB
14 Nov	0920 - Granted GP by Capt Baum-[illegible] Smith		and oriented to Ward by Spc. Fisher. M Janak
	R Walker	22 Nov	Complains of sinus headache and pain in rt side abdomen.
15 Nov	To Personnel Office at their request - Seems to be doing well on G.P. R Walker		
16 Nov	Order written for O. Wd. by Capt Fisher MC - Doing well as Group leader Family. [illegible]		APC Tab. 2 for headache. Dr. Fisher notified of patients other complaint M Janak
18 Nov	Went to finish up 88 + 89's in Main Hosp. Trs. to 27AB R W	23 Nov	Transferred to ward 28 [illegible]

NAME REGISTER NUMBER

KP 27805 A.

YEAR 19

DOCTOR'S ORDERS (CONT'D.)

ORIGINAL ORDERS SIGNED BY DOCTOR. WHEN COPIED, NURSE SIGNS DOCTOR'S AND OWN NAME.

DATE DISC. | DOCTOR'S INITIALS | DATE Dec 4 5 6 7 | SHIFT D E N

4 Dec. C. P. [illegible] by pt. government
noted R Walker [illegible] [illegible] Capt.

9/12 1) Transfer to open ward on 9/12/63
E. Baum Captain

Recopied orders

12 nov ① Stelazine 5 mgm BID — 6 Dec WA
Artane 2 mgm BID — 6 Dec WA

22 nov ② Ornade spans T BID PRN sinus trouble
③ Fiorinal tabs II q4h PRN headache
④ Gastrea antispasmodic 5cc q4h PRN
⑤ Sodium Salicylate 300 mgm tabs II q4h. PRN for arthritic pain.

Dec. Ground pass
E. Baum Captain / [illegible]

6 Dec. 1445 hrs Cmd. [illegible] Chlortrimeton 4 mgm QID x 6 days.
1445 hrs noted [illegible] open ward
William Fisher Capt. M.C.

New Orders

17 Dec. medical consultation [illegible]
neurology consult.
(copied) William Fisher Capt. M.C.
Ornade span T bid PRN sinus trouble
Fiorinal tabs II q4h PRN Headache
Sodium Salicylate 300 mgm [illegible] II q4h PRN
Capt. [illegible]
Allergic to Novocaine + [illegible]

SERVICE NO. 065183 | WARD 26C | AT THE END OF EACH SHIFT, NURSE WHO COMPLETED ORDERS WILL PLACE OWN INITIALS IN PROPER COLUMN. Capt Wm Fisher MC

NAME: STAGNER CLYDE H | GRADE: CPT | REGISTER NO. 6875005 | AGE 39 | DATE OF ADM. 28 Oct 63 | DIAGNOSIS Paranoid Personality

Standard Form 509
(Rev. August 1954)
Bureau of the Budget
Circular A-32

CLINICAL RECORD | **DOCTOR'S PROGRESS NOTES** *(Sign all notes)*

DATE	
28 Nov. 63	Has gone to Col. Tuttle as a reaction to my bruskness earlier this week & took great delight in opening up enough to tell me that "for once it is the environment that is the problem, not me — Col Tuttle agreed that you were in a brusk mood" — an interesting & rather poignant attempt to sort out his projections from reality.
	I suspect he will stay for treatment as long as he ~~[illegible]~~ can pretend he will soon leave.
	[illegible] Capt M.C.
29 Nov	Patient went to Col. Christiansen & told about a head (injury?) in 1951 — not necessarily traumatic, at any rate became dizzy he said & woke up 3 days later. Was told' he said that another one would kill him. Was told he had a brain injury & was given a pneumoencephalogram at Ft Campbell.

(Continued on reverse side)

PATIENT'S IDENTIFICATION (For typed or written entries give: Name—last, first, middle; grade; date; hospital or medical facility) | REGISTER NO. | WARD NO.

STAGNER CLYDE H CPT
6-75 [illegible] 1d3

[illegible] ORGE AH
[illegible] 26CD

DOCTOR'S PROGRESS NOTES
Standard Form 509
509-106

DOCTOR'S PROGRESS NOTES
(*Sign all notes*)

DATE	
	I have discussed this case with Col. Christiansen. We cannot speed up disposition until these records are obtained. Col. Christianson feels he's paranoid too.
	[signature]
2 Dec. 63	After a week of frantically writing letters to congressmen & seeing Col. Christianson (asst commander of hospital) Patient asked my assistance in writing another letter to congressman – ostensibly wanting to know his Dx and time of discharge. He is somewhat more hostile but overall asking for controls – will comply by transferring to Closed ward.
	trans 26 C — William Fisher Capt MC
5 Dec.	Has brought his lawyer into the case – the lawyer seemed, when he talked c̄ me, to ask about the relative financial gains of medical vs. administrative retirement, fewer questions about pts. handling in hosp – pt. has given lawyer a detailed medical Hx which he refused to do c̄ me – pt. invokes an old head injury in 1951 vaguely – will look into this further — W Fisher

U.S. GOVERNMENT PRINTING OFFICE : 1961 O—582552

DOCTOR'S PROGRESS NOTES
Standard Form 509
(Reverse)

Standard Form 509
(Rev. August 1954)
Bureau of the Budget
Circular A-32
509-105

CLINICAL RECORD | **DOCTOR'S PROGRESS NOTES** (*Sign all notes*)

DATE

9 Dec 63 Pt. has experienced another relaxation of his defensiveness after I spent some time c̄ his lawyer last week – also he is going to open ward again. Developed sl. itching c̄ no urticaria on stelazine – meds cut and chlortrimeton added to regimen.

Is expressing again tentative interest in remaining for therapy sl. past 1 Jan "If you don't dig too deep into my personal feelings" – also has expressed some surprise at his wife's writing me, thru social service a couple of weeks ago to tell of her concerns about his veiled self-destructive ideas.

In reviewing his old records I find it remarkable the intensity of his ability to cause discord among the staff at hospitals and to invoke famous senators & descrepancies between Army Regulations and US law –

Also there is Hx of a single ? siezure in 1951 which was well worked up & nothing found. Pt has been somewhat inappropriate since 1952 but not really paranoid in marked degree til last few years. – He would be a challenge (and a trial to treat.) William Fisher Capt MC

(Continue on reverse side)

PATIENT'S IDENTIFICATION (For typed or written entries give: Name—last, first, middle; grade; date; hospital or medical facility) | REGISTER NO. | WARD NO.

Stagner, Clyde

DOCTOR'S PROGRESS NOTES
Standard Form 509
509-105

DOCTOR'S PROGRESS NOTES
(*Sign all notes*)

DATE	
14 Dec.	a repeat call from pts lawyer who continues to express concern whether further Rx would decrease pts. disability rating by PEB & hence make financial considerations involved in whether pt. stays for further Rx — I said that financially pt would be better off if he is adequately functioning in society & that the degree of impairment on admission was strongly considered in the final PEB determination, especially since I do not anticipate even remotely an opportunity for more than a beginning therapy — hopefully enough to allow pt to experience its benefits & obtain further Rx later —
	another concern expressed by lawyer was regarding my gathering childhood history — pt. has repeatedly assured me his was "normal" and refuses to elaborate — lawyer noted the same attitude in pt. — I pointed out to lawyer that early memories (meaningful ones) may occur as a byproduct of successful therapeutic intervention & that quizzing pt. re these would meet only c̄ conventional, "happy family" type responses — no significant data —
	I have been communicating c̄ lawyer c̄ pt's full verbal assent & feel this sort of

U.S. GOVERNMENT PRINTING OFFICE : 1959 O—530184

DOCTOR'S PROGRESS NOTES
Standard Form 509
(Reverse)

Standard Form 509
(Rev. August 1954)
Bureau of the Budget
Circular A-32
509-105

CLINICAL RECORD | **DOCTOR'S PROGRESS NOTES**
(Sign all notes)

DATE	
14 Dec 63 (cont'd)	mutual trust will eventually be most helpful for pt.
	He (pt.) is very concerned & emotionally involved c wife again via mail - I showed him a letter from her in which she expressed great concern about his being depressed; he was surprised she cared.
	He will take a leave over the holidays & I have advised both to come back & engage in a family therapy of at least brief duration.
	W. Fisher Capt M.C.
19 Jan	2 wk leave over Christmas - final summary dictated for PEB - pt. wants to stay after PEB - generally much more relaxed. Has a job - in the small claims office of the JAG.
	W. Fisher Capt M.C.
30 Jan	medical board concurs in psychotic diagnosis Will refer to PEB.
	W. Fisher Capt M.C.
19 Feb.	Doing well - slight administrative delay in getting pt. to PEB, he tolerated the delay well.
	W. Fisher Capt M.C.

(Continue on reverse side)

PATIENT'S IDENTIFICATION (*For typed or written entries give: Name—last, first, middle; grade; date; hospital or medical facility*) | REGISTER NO. | WARD NO.

DOCTOR'S PROGRESS NOTES
Standard Form 509
509-105

KENNETH A. ROBERTS
AT LARGE, ALABAMA

DISTRICT OFFICE:
FEDERAL BUILDING
ANNISTON, ALABAMA

COMMITTEE:
INTERSTATE AND FOREIGN COMMERCE

CHAIRMAN, SUBCOMMITTEE:
PUBLIC HEALTH AND SAFETY

Congress of the United States
House of Representatives
Washington, D. C.

October 24, 1963

Captain Clyde H. Stagner
Mil. Art. Div
USA Cml School
Fort McClellan, Alabama

Dear Captain Stagner:

Thank you for your recent letter regarding your hospitalization at Fort McClellan, Alabama.

I can certainly understand and sympathize with your situation and will be happy to contact the Department of the Army in your behalf. Just as soon as information can be received, I will further advise you.

With every good and kind wish, I am

Very sincerely,

Kenneth A. Roberts
Kenneth A. Roberts

KAR:wwg

CERTIFICATE OF RETIREMENT

FROM THE ARMED FORCES OF THE UNITED STATES OF AMERICA

TO ALL WHO SHALL SEE THESE PRESENTS, GREETING:

THIS IS TO CERTIFY THAT

Clyde U Stagner 065 103

Captain Chemical Corps

HAVING SERVED FAITHFULLY AND HONORABLY,
WAS RETIRED FROM THE

UNITED STATES ARMY

ON THE first DAY OF May
ONE THOUSAND NINE HUNDRED AND Sixty-four

WASHINGTON, D. C.

J. C. Lambert
MAJOR GENERAL, UNITED STATES ARMY,
THE ADJUTANT GENERAL

DD FORM 363A, 1 AUG 63

SPECIAL ORDERS)
)
NUMBER 101)

HEADQUARTERS
DEPARTMENT OF THE ARMY
Washington, D.C., 23 April 1964

*** * ***

155. TC 440. CWO, W-2 RAYMOND, L. GREER W21455439 QMC having been determined to be perm unfit for dy by reason of phys disab of 50 percent incurred while entitled to rec basic pay is ret fr active svc with gr and ret pay of CWO, W-2, as prov by title 10 US Code secs 1201 and 1372. He is rel fr asg Med Holding Co Valley Forge GH, Phoenixville, Pa. EDCSA 30 Apr 1964 and placed on AUS ret list 1 May 1964. HOSTWOY. PCS. TDN. PPSIA. 2142010 01-1731-1732-1733-1735-1735-1736 P1517 S99-999. SPN 563.

*** * ***

172. TC 433. CWO, W-2 DELMAR J. DAVIS W2153167 (CWO, W-3, USAR) upon his appl is ret fr active svc in the grade of CWO, W-3 under prov title 10 US Code sec 1293 after more than 20 yrs active Fed svc. He is rel fr asg and dy, Phoenixville, Pa, EDCSA 30 Jun 1964 and placed on AUS USA ret list 1 Jul 1964. On 1 Jul 1964 he is trf to USAR (Ret Res) and asg to USARCEN, St Louis 32, Mo. HOSTWOY. PCS. TDN. PPSIA. 2142010 01-1731-1732-1733-1735-1736-1737 P1517 S99-999.

*** * ***

173. TC 440. CAPT CLYDE H. STAGNER 065183 Cml C Having been determined to be perm unfit for dy by reason of phys disability of 30 percent incurred while entitled to rec basic pay is ret fr active svc with gr and ret pay of Capt as prov by title 10 US Code secs 1201 and 1372. He is rel fr asg Med Holding Co Valley Forge Gen Hosp, Phoenixville, Pa. EDCSA 30 Apr 1964 and placed on USA ret list 1 May 1964. HOSTWOY. PCS. TDN. PPSIA. 2142010 01-1731-1732-1733-1735-1736-1737 P1517 S99-999. SPN 563.

*** * ***

274. TC 444. UP 10 US Code 1202 FNE having been detm to be unfit for dy by reason of phys disab is rel asg and dy on EDCSA at sta indc and on day fol EDCSA is placed on temp disab ret list in gr indc. HOSTWOY. PCS. TDN. PPSIA. 2142010 01-1761-1763 P1517 S99-999. SPN 270.

*** * ***

ROHBROUGH, DANA M., PFC (E-3) RA24416203 MOS 411.10 Med Holding Co Valley Forge GH, Phoenixville, Pa.
Place of retirement: Weston, WVa. Retired grade and SN: Sgt (E-5)
Disab rating (percent): 30 Date retired: 1 May 1964 EDCSA: 30 Apr 1964

*** * ***

BY ORDER OF THE SECRETARY OF THE ARMY:

EARLE G. WHEELER,
General, United States Army,
Chief of Staff.

Official:
J.C. LAMBERT,
Major General, United States Army,
Adjutant

A TRUE COPY:

ANGELO J TROISI
Capt, MSC

DISTRIBUTION: 120 cys Trf Pt; 150 cys Off Sec; 3 cys MHCo (3416); 2 cys Finance; 1 cy ea: Supply, Trans, Registrar, C Tng Br, Adj's Off, Post Off, MR Unit, Mil Per Br, Msg Ctr, 15 cys Orders Sec.

(Sign all notes)

DATE	
29 Oct 63	Patient charming, cooperative (superficially) this AM and would like to get off closed ward. For mental status see note above.
	Dx: Paranoid Personality c̄ Dr. Fisher
	Rec: ① Contact Fort McClellan to determine reason patient was sent here.
	② Determine if you then need patient assigned.
	W. D. Boyleton, Capt MC

CLINICAL RECORD | **PHYSICAL EXAMINATION**

DATE OF EXAM.	HEIGHT	WEIGHT AVERAGE	WEIGHT MAXIMUM	WEIGHT PRESENT	TEMPERATURE	PULSE	BLOOD PRESSURE
29 Oct 63	5-11			180	98⁶	84	128/74

INSTRUCTIONS.—Describe (1) General Appearance and Mental Status; (2) Head and Neck (General); (3) Eyes; (4) Ears; (5) Nose; (6) Mouth; (7) Throat; (8) Teeth; (9) Chest (General); (10) Lungs; (11) Cardiovascular; (12) Abdomen; (13) Hernia; (14) Genitalia; (15) Rectum; (16) Prostate; (17) Back; (18) Extremities; (19) Neurological; (20) Skin; (21) Lymphatics.

A W.D., W.N., W.M. c̄ a haughty, hostile, evasive approach. He is fully oriented & superficially cooperative but not answering any meaningful questions while "under duress." No delusions or hallucinations, but highly inappropriate behavior — "I am here to get a psychiatric evaluation but I refuse to talk while under duress." Apparently being in a psychiatric hospital is duress. He also seems prepared to bargain and negotiate for privileges in return for information he might divulge

64

ENLISTED RECORD AND REPORT OF SEPARATION
HONORABLE DISCHARGE

1. Last name - First name - Middle initial: STAGNER CLYDE H
2. Army serial no.: 36 753 278
3. Grade: TEC 4
4. Arm or service: ORD
5. Component: AUS
6. Organization: 1193 SCU (USMAP) ARMY TRNG SCH
7. Date of separation: 6 FEB 46
8. Place of separation: SEPARATION CENTER CAMP GRANT ILL
9. Permanent address for mailing purposes: 609 HENRY ST JOLIET ILL
10. Date of birth: 27 JUL 1924
11. Place of birth: SUMMIT ILL
12. Address from which employment will be sought: SEE 9
13. Color eyes: HAZEL
14. Color hair: BROWN
15. Height: 5' 11"
16. Weight: 164 lbs.
17. No. depend.: 0
18. Race: White X
19. Marital status: Single X
20. U.S. Citizen: X
21. Civilian occupation and no.: FOREMAN 5-91.872

MILITARY HISTORY

22. Date of induction: 11 JUN 43
23. Date of enlistment:
24. Date of entry into active service: 11 JUN 43
25. Place of entry into service: CHICAGO ILL
26. Selective service data — Registered: Yes X
27. Local S.S. Board no.: 1
28. County and State: WILL CO ILL
29. Home address at time of entry into service: SEE 9
30. Military occupational specialty and no.: AMMUNITION RENOVATOR 949
31. Military qualification and date: MM W/RIFLE
32. Battles and campaigns: NEW GUINEA
33. Decorations and citations: 2 OVERSEAS SERVICE BARS AMERICAN CAMPAIGN MEDAL ASIATIC-PACIFIC CAMPAIGN MEDAL W/1 BRONZE BATTLE STAR GOOD CONDUCT MEDAL WORLD WAR II VICTORY MEDAL-
34. Wounds received in action: NONE
35. Latest immunization dates: Smallpox JUL 44 IMM; Typhoid JUL 45 ST; Tetanus JUL 44 ST; Other (specify):
36. Service outside continental U.S. and return:

Date of departure	Destination	Date of arrival
18 NOV 44	PTO	11 DEC 44
1 SEPT 45	USA	3 SEPT 45

37. Total length of service: Continental service — Years 1, Months 7, Days 10; Foreign service — Years 0, Months 11, Days 16
38. Highest grade held: TEC 4
39. Prior service: NONE
40. Reason and authority for separation: CONV OF GOVT RR 1-1 (DEMOBILIZATION) AR 615-365 DATED 15 DEC 44
41. Service schools attended: ARMY TRAINING SCHOOL AMHERST COLLEGE AMHERST MASS
42. Education (Years): Grammar 8, High School 4, College 0

PAY DATA VOO 822424

43. Longevity for pay purposes: Years 2, Months 7, Days 26
44. Mustering out pay: Total $300, This payment $100
45. Soldier deposits: $20.61
46. Travel pay: $6.25
47. Total amount, name of disbursing officer: $163.86 G F DOLBEAR CAPT FD

INSURANCE NOTICE

IMPORTANT: If premium is not paid when due or within thirty-one days thereafter, insurance will lapse. Make checks or money orders payable to the Treasurer of the U.S. and forward to Collections Subdivision, Veterans Administration, Washington 25, D.C.

48. Kind of insurance: Nat. Serv. X
49. How paid: Allotment X
50. Effective date of allotment discontinuance: 28 FEB 46
51. Date of next premium due (One month after 50): 31 MAR 46
52. Premium due each month: $6.50
53. Intention of veteran to: Continue X; Discontinue X

54. Right thumb print

55. Remarks (This space for completion of above items or entry of other items specified in W. D. Directives):
* AMHERST COLLEGE
LAPEL BUTTON ISSUED ASR SCORE (2 SEPT 45) 41

56. Signature of person being separated: Clyde H. Stagner
57. Personnel officer (Type name, grade and organization - signature): JOHANNA M LOUWERENS 2ND LT WAC

WD AGO Form 53-55, 1 November 1944. This form supersedes all previous editions of WD AGO Forms 53 and 55 for enlisted persons entitled to an Honorable Discharge, which will not be used after receipt of this revision.

APPLICATION FOR READJUSTMENT ALLOWANCE, PUBLIC LAW 346, MADE THROUGH Joliet, STATE Illinois

4. DEPARTMENT, COMPONENT AND BRANCH OR CLASS: ARMY-RA-CML C
5. PLACE OF BIRTH (City and State or Country): Summit Illinois
6. DATE OF BIRTH: DAY 27

7a. RACE: Caucasian
b. SEX: M
8. U.S. CITIZEN: YES
9. MARITAL STATUS: Married
d. WEIGHT: 185

10a. HIGHEST CIVILIAN EDUCATION LEVEL ATTAINED: 2 yr College Level
b. MAJOR/COURSE OR FIELD: Col Battery (GED) & Physics

11a. TYPE OF TRANSFER OR DISCHARGE: Retired
b. STATION OR INSTALLATION AT WHICH EFFECTED: Valley Forge General Hospital Phoenixville Pa
c. REASON AND AUTHORITY: Retirement Permanent Disability Title 10 United States Code secs 1201 and 1372 SPN 563
d. EFFECTIVE DATE: DAY 30 MONTH Apr YEAR 64

12. LAST DUTY ASSIGNMENT AND MAJOR COMMAND: HHCTrpComdUSACmlCen&Sch(3A-3178)FtMcClmAla
13a. CHARACTER OF SERVICE: HONORABLE
b. TYPE OF CERTIFICATE ISSUED: DD Form 363A

14. SELECTIVE SERVICE NUMBER: NA
15. SELECTIVE SERVICE LOCAL BOARD NUMBER, CITY, COUNTY AND STATE: NA
16. DATE INDUCTED: NA

17. DISTRICT OR AREA COMMAND TO WHICH RESERVIST TRANSFERRED: NA

18. TERMINAL DATE OF RESERVE OBLIGATION: NA
19. CURRENT ACTIVE SERVICE OTHER THAN BY INDUCTION
a. SOURCE OF ENTRY: ☐ ENLISTED (First Enlistment) ☐ ENLISTED (Prior Service) ☐ REENLISTED ☒ OTHER Ordered from USAR's
b. TERM OF SERVICE (Years): NA
c. DATE OF ENTRY: DAY 26 MONTH Feb YEAR 49

20. PRIOR REGULAR ENLISTMENTS: NA
21. GRADE, RATE OR RANK AT TIME OF ENTRY INTO CURRENT ACTIVE SERVICE: 2d Lt
22. PLACE OF ENTRY INTO CURRENT ACTIVE SERVICE (City and State): Joliet Illinois

23. HOME OF RECORD AT TIME OF ENTRY INTO ACTIVE SERVICE (Street, RFD, City, County and State): Joliet Illinois

24. STATEMENT OF SERVICE

		YEARS	MONTHS	DAYS
a. CREDITABLE FOR BASIC PAY PURPOSES	(1) NET SERVICE THIS PERIOD	15	2	5
	(2) OTHER SERVICE	2	10	19
	(3) TOTAL (Line (1) + line (2))	18	0	24
b. TOTAL ACTIVE SERVICE		18	0	1
c. FOREIGN AND/OR SEA SERVICE		5	11	21

25. MOS NUMBER AND TITLE: 67330 Instr Nuclear Wpns
RELATED CIVILIAN OCCUPATION AND D.O.T. NUMBER: Physicist 0-35.73

26. DECORATIONS, MEDALS, BADGES, COMMENDATIONS, CITATIONS AND CAMPAIGN RIBBONS AWARDED OR AUTHORIZED: Army of Occupation Medal Expert Infantry Badge National Defense Service Medal

27. WOUNDS RECEIVED AS A RESULT OF ACTION WITH ENEMY FORCES (Place and date, if known): NA

28. SERVICE SCHOOLS OR COLLEGES, COLLEGE TRAINING COURSES AND/OR POST-GRADUATE COURSES SUCCESSFULLY COMPLETED

SCHOOL OR COURSE a	DATES (From-To) b	MAJOR COURSES c
Trans School	3 months 1949	Sp AssocBasic O Crs
Inf Sch	15 weeks 1952	Assoc Trans CO Crs
Trans Sch	10 months 1957	TOAC #10
USA CmlC Sch	4 weeks 1960	Fld Gr Off Ref Crs
USA CmlC Sch	2 weeks 1962	Radl Safety Crs
CivDefStaffColl BCMich	July 1962	Radiological InstrCrse

29. OTHER SERVICE TRAINING COURSES SUCCESSFULLY COMPLETED: None

30a. GOVERNMENT LIFE INSURANCE IN FORCE: ☒ YES ☐ NO
b. AMOUNT OF ALLOTMENT: $7.90
c. MONTH ALLOTMENT DISCONTINUED: May '64

31a. VA BENEFITS PREVIOUSLY APPLIED FOR (Specify type): Education
b. VA CLAIM NUMBER: C- Unknown

32. REMARKS
No time lost under 10 USC 972
Par 10 AR601-210 applies
Item 3a temp Captain AUS aptd 29 Mar 54 perm Captain RA aptd 16 Nov 56
Lump sum payment made for 60 days accrued leave SSAN: 349-12-3030
Blood Group "O" Separated for permanent disability retirement
Disability 30 percent

33. PERMANENT ADDRESS FOR MAILING PURPOSES AFTER TRANSFER OR DISCHARGE (Street, RFD, City, County and State): 147 N Hamilton St Lockport(WillCo) Illinois
34. SIGNATURE OF PERSON BEING TRANSFERRED OR DISCHARGED: Clyde H Stegner

35a. TYPED NAME, GRADE AND TITLE OF AUTHORIZING OFFICER: ANGELO J TROISI CAPTAIN MSC ASST ADJUTANT
b. SIGNATURE OF OFFICER AUTHORIZED TO SIGN

DD FORM 1 NOV 55 214 — REPLACES EDITION OF 1 JUL 53, WHICH IS OBSOLETE. ARMED FORCES OF THE UNITED STATES REPORT OF TRANSFER OR DISCHARGE 1

ALABAMA WING
ANNISTON SQUADRON
CIVIL AIR PATROL
U S AIR FORCE AUX.

January 7, 1963

Subject: Appreciation

To: Commandant, U. S. Army Chemical Corps School, Fort McClellan, Alabama

1. On Saturday and Sunday, 29-30 December 1962, several members of your Staff and Faculty conducted a 14-hour course of instruction in radiological survey, particularly by air, for selected members of the Alabama Wing, Civil Air Patrol and Calhoun County Civil Defense personnel. In addition to having been the designated CAP project officer for this course of instruction, I was privileged to attend your school those two days.

2. Unfortunately, several deferents prevented full attendance as we had planned and thus the class could have included many more deserving students. This is sincerely regreted but apparently could not be foreseen.

3. We were highly impressed with the planning, scheduling and conduct of this short course. The administrative arrangements, to include transportation, housing, rations and social contacts, were excellent. The quality of instruction, to include preparation of the instructors, training aids and facilities was outstanding. We were particularly pleased with the superior performances of our instructors, Major Stafford R. Brooke, Jr., Captain Clyde H. Stagner, and Captain Willis S. Rosing, Jr. Their enthusiasm and capabilities left nothing to be desired and were even more noteworthy considering that this fourteen hours of instruction was conducted during what might have otherwise been a holiday week-end. Captain Stagner, as Course Director, was most solicitous for our welfare and diligent in his preparation for and conduet of the instruction.

4. We are most appreciative of the fine course your school conducted for us and anticipate an opportunity to reciprocate.

Jack M. Williams

Jack M. Williams
Commander, Major

cc: Alabama Wing CAP

Capt W. D. Wessels
US Army Chemical Corps School
Fort McClellan Ala USA
11 Jan 63

Dear Lt Col [illegible]

I am introducing Capt Clyde Stagner. US Army Chemical Corps RA. who is a personal friend of mine and with whom I have had the pleasure of knowing academically and socially.

I feel sure that you will have time to speak with Capt Stagner in conjunction with my work and also he may arrive in Washington in time to enjoy the Australian hospitality at the [illegible]

Kindest regards

[illegible signature]

Lt Col W.P.C [illegible]
Office of the Military Attaché
2001 Connecticut Ave
Washington D.C.

Office of the
COMMANDANT
AJMCL-C

30 January 1964

SUBJECT: Certificate of Commendation

THRU: Commanding General
Valley Forge General Hospital
Phoenixville, Pennsylvania

TO: Captain Clyde H. Stagner
Valley Forge General Hospital
Phoenixville, Pennsylvania

1. I am pleased to pass on to you this Certificate of Commendation from Lieutenant General M. J. Asensio, Director, New York State Civil Defense Commission for the outstanding assistance you rendered to personnel of the New York State Civil Defense Commission.

2. The complimentary comments indicate not only your high level of professional competency, but an ability to perform in a very effective manner with other installations. Thank you for a job well done.

1 Incl
as

L. A. PARKS
Colonel, CmlC
Commandant

New York State
Civil Defense Commission

Certificate of Commendation

awarded to

Captain Clyde Stagner

In recognition and appreciation of meritorious, patriotic and dedicated service to Civil Defense.

[signature]
State Director

Dated this 22nd day of January 1964

STATE OF NEW YORK
EXECUTIVE DEPARTMENT

NEW YORK STATE CIVIL DEFENSE COMMISSION

162 WASHINGTON AVENUE
ALBANY 10, N. Y.

LT. GEN. F. W. FARRELL
DIRECTOR

1 February 1963

Colonel Laverne A. Parks, Commandant
U.S. Army Chemical Corps School
Fort McClellan, Alabama

Dear Colonel Parks:

I wish to commend two of your officers, Captain Clyde Stagner and Lt. Robert Breedlove, for the outstanding lectures they delivered recently before the New York State Radiological Chiefs in Albany, New York. The material they presented on aerial radiological surveys was well organized and delivered in a highly effective manner.

Thank you for your assistance in making our meeting most educational and informative. If this office can reciprocate in any way, please let me know.

Sincerely,

F. W. FARRELL
Director

U.S. ARMY CHEMICAL CORPS SCHOOL
FORT McCLELLAN, ALABAMA

IN REPLY REFER TO:
AJMCL-T

24 January 1963

SUBJECT: Letter of Appreciation

THRU: Chief, Radiological Branch
Technical Division
US Army Chemical Corps School
Fort McClellan, Alabama

TO: Captain Clyde H. Stagner
Radiological Branch
Technical Division
US Army Chemical Corps School
Fort McClellan, Alabama

It is a pleasure for me to forward the attached copy of a letter of appreciation from the Sixth Naval District for your co-operation with respect to the INDMAN SIX Mobile Radiac Repair Facility. Your efforts in this matter reflect credit on the School, Technical Division, and yourself.

Roy H Berger
ROY H. BERGER
Lt Colonel, CmlC
Chief, Technical Division

1 Incl
as

Incl 10

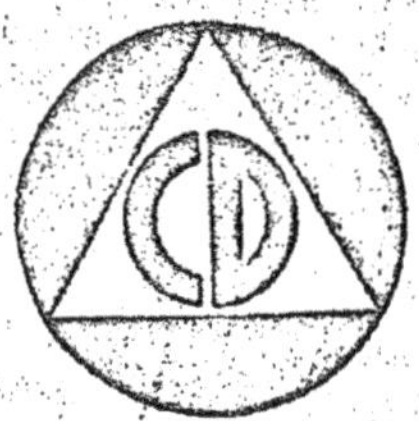

CO-ORDINATOR OF

CALHOUN COUNTY
CIVIL DEFENSE DEPARTMENT
ANNISTON, ALABAMA

S. J. JONES
PHONE AD XXXXX
7-4731

February 12, 1963

The Commandant
U. S. Army Chemical Corps School
Fort McClellan, Alabama

Dear Sir:

We are enclosing Certificates of Appreciation for Major S. R. Brooke, Captain C. H. Stagner, and Captain W. S. Rosing for their outstanding service of instruction in the recent Radiological Survey Training Course at Fort McClellan.

We will appreciate your seeing that these Officers receive their Certificates.

Sincerely yours,

S. J. Jones

S. J. Jones
Coordinator

SJJ:bp

Enclosures

U. S. ARMY CHEMICAL CENTER AND SCHOOL
Fort McClellan, Alabama

LO 55 29 July 1963

SUBJECT: CBR Proficiency Test Task Team

TO: See Distribution

1. TC 350. Fol indiv this sta APPOINTED.

COTTINGHAM, HARRY H 0330599 LT COL CmlC HHC Trp Comd USA Cml Cen & Sch (3178)
Team Chief (Add dy)
LONGSTREET, JOHN M 068132 MAJ CmlC HHC Trp Comd USA Cml Cen & Sch (3178)
Action Off (Add dy)
STAGNER, CLYDE H 065183 CAPT CmlC HHC Trp Comd USA Cml Cen & Sch (3178)
Nuc Wpns Eff Engr & Recorder
Apt to: CBR Proficiency Test Task Team
Eff date: 24 Jul 63
Pd: Indef
Purpose: To prepare the CBR Proficiency Test for FY 65, which CONARC will administer throughout CONUS.
Auth: VOCO
Sp instr: The team will write, compose expermental test and arrange for publication, convene and brief the test administration and evaluators as designated by CONARC.
VOCO date cfm: 24 Jul 63

FOR THE COMMANDANT:

OFFICIAL:

PERRY E. SEMAN
CWO W-4, USA
Asst Secretary

G. H. ROBERTS
Lt Colonel, CmlC
Secretary

DISTRIBUTION:
10-UPO Trp Comd USA Cml Cen & Sch
5-CO, HHC Trp Comd USA Cml Cen & Sch
2-CO, Trp Comd USA Cml Cen & Sch
2-Ea indiv conc
1-Orders clerk
2-Central files

CHAPTER 3

TIMELINE

1968.

Stagner`s attempt to acquaint several Veteran` s Administration medical doctors about the Sojourner Resolution was immediately met with, "Forget the whole thing !" A Special NP examination by the VA Outpatient was conducted on August 29, 1968.

Stagner met Virginia Romano, a widow with six children, whom he married on May 1.,1968, and in 1969, adopted her five youngest children. Prior to the marriage, Stagner apprised Virginia of the Sojourner Resolution and his subsequent experiences which were in, and would remain in, his conscience "backpack". A year after the marriage, Stagner`s son ,Joseph, joined the family. Two years after ,his son, Mark , joined.

After working in radiation evaluations for the Pinellas County Health Department since 1966, and being appointed a consultant to the United States Bureau of Radiological Health, Stagner went back to college. He graduated in Dec,1970, with a Bachelor of Science in Engineering, Energy Conversion.

1975.

With Virginia`s assistance, an allegorical fictional manuscript entitled, "The Muted Bugle", relating to the Sojourner Resolution ,was submitted for movie scripts but the effort was unsuccessful. One writer wrote that he was afraid to get involved although he was sympathetic to the effort: another met Stagner in a St. Petersburg`s bowling alley but later failed to produce a script. With daughter, Rama Laurie, involved, the manuscript was deposited with the screen writer`s guild.

1976.

Circa 1976, Stagner made an appointment with the FBI in St. Petersburg, Florida. Arriving in the downtown Federal Office Building, Stagner was escorted by a young suited agent into an office with several desks with protruding large black cables. Stagner advised the young man of the Sojourner Resolution with its multiple destinations in the United States. No names were mentioned. The agent asked no questions, advised Stagner they were just involved in politics, followed by an escort to the exit, "*THE AGENT DID NOT DENY THE EXISTANCE OF THE SOJOUNER RESOLUTION".*

Circa 1976, a telephone call was placed to someone at 1-202-224-1700. Stagner believed he was calling the Senate Intelligence Committee. The result was a demand for the name source of the telephone number. His response to the mentioning of a treasonous group in Alexandria across the Potomac was disdain before he hung up.

1990.

Stagner`s daughter, Rama Laurie, who was involved in the ,"Muted Bugle", effort of 1975, separated the marital theme from the assassination theme, and wrote her first movie script entitled ,"Blue Sky". The title was named after the U.S. Army

award presented to Capt. Stagner for his innovative technical contributions to the national defense effort.. The script was purchased for a full screen movie starring Jessica Lange who won a best actress Oscar for playing Rama Laurie`s mother. Tommy Lee Jones played the male lead. Stagner was hired as the nuclear effects advisor and went on location in Selma ,Alabama in April, 1990. At a several hour staff session, one of the ten members present asked Stagner about the Kennedy assassination to which Stagner answered,

" That information is in the manuscript, 'Muted Bugle', on file with the Screen Writers Guild. That is all I have to say, *"they all knew the background of the movie being put together".*

During the first week of May, 1990, Stagner, Rama Laurie, and the other two writers met for a three hour evening meeting with the Director, Tony Richardson, in his Hollywood Hills residence. Filming began the following week: Richardson knew the character the male lead was to play. Although filming was completed in July, the movie was put on a shelf because of Orion`s dire financial situation.

1992.

With the election of President Clinton, Stagner`s apprehension, concerning a repeat performance of the Sojourner Resolution, increased. Stagner found a nearby location where, for $300, he was administered a polygraph by a reputable provider. The results of the polygraph substantiated Stagner`s citation of treason. His sole purpose in taking the polygraph was to prevent, if possible, a repeat of a similar November 22, 1963 event. The assessment of politics to the Sojourner Resolution is not supported by the polygraph. The word, "politically", does not appear before the word, "opposing", in the polygraph question nor was the word, "opposing" or any derivation thereof, read in the Sojourner Resolution presented at Fort McClellan in the fall of 1962.

President Kennedy had not reached mid term in the fall of 1962, *"who would be in political opposition against him before mid term".* In any case, political opposition in the fall of 1962 against President Kennedy, by his subordinate Officers of the U.S. military forces , would be treasonous. The President of the United States Of America appoints both Reserve and Regular military officers to include obedience to his orders, and to those orders of future Presidents of the United States. Copies of the polygraph were sent to several agencies and persons of interest including U.S. Senator DeConcini, a member of the Select Intelligence Committee. One of his aids, after consulting with the local Veterans Administration, returned the effort with a telephone call to Stagner, with,

"If the VA ever tries to take away your disability, call us."Stagner mused, *"in this case the polygraph is a boomerang for the VA".*

On October 16,1992, Stagner requested Senator DeConcini`s assistance in changing Stagner`s incorrect VA cited diagnosis of Paranoid Schizophrenic back to the U.S.Army`s Paranoid: suspiciousness. This change in diagnosis was done in 1964 in the Chicago Veterans Administration Regional Office, VARO, by some one other than a medical doctor and in the absence of a VA doctor`s medical diagnosis.

This change occurred upon receipt of Stagner`s military medical records from the Valley Forge General Hospital. Stagner was never in the Chicago VARO. On Nov 10, 1992, he requested the VA to correct their error.

On Nov 11, 1992, a VA confusing letter was received confirming Stagner`s accusation. Stagner, on Feb 10,1993, received another letter from the VA advising him of his option to request the VA to make a diagnostic change, *"the VA could not correct their own error without a patient` s request. How many of their errors has the VA corrected".*

1994.

In August 1994, the world premier of the movie, "Blue Sky", in the Lincoln Center, New York City, was attended by Stagner and his daughters. Rama Laurie Stagner, introduced as a principal by actress Jody Foster , stood to a full house applause. Following the premier showing ,Orion Pictures invited all the Stagners to a dinner/dance at the Tavern on the Green where Bon Jovi ,and others , entertained. In October, 1994, the Arizona Daily Star published a feature story, "Soulful view of human nature; movie captured Tucsonan`s ordeal", by Tom Turner. Although the large Davis Monthan Air Force Base is located in Tucson, Stagner was never asked one question in Tucson, or elsewhere, about his objection, to the proposed officer opposition to President Kennedy, which was mentioned in the newspaper article. Stagner`s retired military friends accepted the statement as if anticipated although occasionally one of the six bums would refer to Stagner " as the soldier who wintered at Valley Forge".

2004.

On December 10. 2002, a VA document displayed a disability rating of Pyschosis Shiz Para DX Code 92133 for Stagner. On April 24, 2004, a request was submitted for the VA Inspector General`s assistance in correcting his erroneous diagnosis.

Daughter Ginny Huston welded together a family reunion for Las Vegas in August, 2004, to celebrate Stagner`s 80th birthday. Dr. James(Jim) Callan, M.D., informed Ginny that he and his wife would attend. Stagner raised Jim Callan from the age of three to fifteen as a stepson inhis first marriage. Jim was a good natured, good looking towhead who was a plus in everything. Stagner wanted to balance the theme of the movie, "Blue Sky", with other resultant causations leading to similar conclusions. At the reunion, a letter addressed to Jim, and his wife, Jeannie, was given to him and distributed to each of Stagner`s living children. Late the following morning, Jim presented Stagner with a book, "Rise To Rebellion" ,by Jeff Shaara. Opening the book, Stagner read, "Happy Birthday,Dad". Later, in Tucson, Stagner discovered the book included John Adam`s defense of a British Captain and Soldiers in a precusor to the Revolutionary War even though Adams was an adamant revolutionary.

VA OUTPATIENT CLINIC 516/136B:ev
St. Petersburg, Florida
August 29, 1968

SPECIAL NP EXAMINATION

HISTORY: This patient is an adult white male, well developed and well nourished, age 44, married, a widower May of 1968. There are six step-children to this union, ages 14, 13, 11, 10, 6 and 4. He was divorced in 1965, lived with this wife 16 years. He was divorced from this wife for a period of four months and again they reunited. He has five children by this union, ages 18, 16, 14, 10 and 11, and one stepchild who is an adult. These children are with the mother in Fresno, California. He states that she has not remarried.

He has been in Florida since 1965 coming from California. He states his wife owns their home.

Form 21-2507 dated 5/13/68 indicates service connection paranoid state (competent); cirrhosis of the liver; gouty arthritis with hyperuricemia;allergic rhinitis with history of maxillary sinusitis; bronchitis; urinary tract infection (by history); and hemorrhoids; purpose of examination other,RF.

Family history: Is essentially negative.
Childhood diseases: Had the usual childhood illnesses.
Adult diseases: Denies venereal disease.
States he had service in the Army 6/11/43 to 2/6/46. He was in the Ordnance. States he volunteered for the draft at the age of 18. He incurred no gunshot wounds or high explosive shell wounds during service. No major operative procedures. Was hospitalized during his first tour of duty in New Guinea for swollen glands for about a month. Was returned to duty and discharged from Camp Grant, Illinois, Discharge Center. He had no hospitalization periods prior to his discharge nor prior to his reinlistment 2/6/49. He had continual service from that date until 5/1/64. He was last hospitalized at Valley Forge General Hospital prior to his retirement. He was retired medically as a captain.

Since service in 1964 he was hospitalized at the VA Hospital, San Francisco, Calif. for two days in June of 1965 for cystoscopic examination. No other hospitalization periods to date.

Schooling: Graduated from high school. States he is presently planning to go to the University of South Florida under the GI Bill.

Habits: Smokes two packs of cigarettes a day. Does not use whiskey. Apparently

STAGNER, Clyde Hurchell C-14 073 858

he had used some excessively during service. He drinks two cans of beer a day.

Occupation: Prior to service was a student and was a plant worker in a munitions factory. 1946 to 1949 he went to college for two years under the GI Bill and then worked in an amunition factory for one year. Since service he has been under Vocational Rehabilitation, 1964 and 1965, and came to Florida in May of 1966. Presently he is working for the Pinellas Health Department in the radiation department. Has been there since 5/66 and plans to remain until 9/30/68 and then return to school. He states he is receiving for this work $560 a month. He refuses to state the amount of his retired pay. States he gets no VA compensation.

PRESENT COMPLAINTS: "No, I am not sick. No, I have no aches or pains today. I ache quite frequently in all my joints."

MENTAL EXAMINATION: This patient is neat and tidy about his person. He remains pleasant and cooperative throughout the interview. However, there are times that he is more or less definitely suspicious of what is said and how the questions are meant for him. During this interview there is no evidence of him being hallucinated, definitely delusional or having any definite paranoid ideation as such. During the first portion of the interview his questions were given in short, quick answers. However, after full rapport was established he became more free in his production. He tells the story of an apparent or alleged conspiracy against the President of the United States when in the service in Germany and states that he is willing to go under Sodium Pentothal to have with him at the time his wife and a lawyer to prove that he was correct in what he was allegedly charged with. This patient this date is fully oriented and in contact with his surroundings. His memory for past and recent events, his retention and immediate recall are excellent. His general knowledge is commensurate with his educational advantages. The ideas that he has relative to his service and the difficulties in it are well fixed. There is no paranoid ideation expressed concerning others nor is there any evidence of suicidal or homicidal intent. This patient is fully oriented and in contact with his surroundings definitely mentally alert, his memory for past and recent events, his retention and immediate recall show no impairment. Apparently enjoys matching wits with the examiner. There was no suspiciousness on the part of the patient toward this examiner noted during the interview. Throughout the interview there are no definite affective disorders or display. His affect is in accordance with his mood, he remaining generally pleasant and cooperative. There is no emotional flattening or instability at this writing. In this examiner's opinion this patient presents insufficient findings to warrant a diagnois of any one type of schizophrenia nor are there any definitely well systematized delusional material in general found. The ideation had at the time of this patient's difficulty in the service still remains the same, he unchanging his thinking about it. He was advised relative to having him submit to Sodium Pentothal narcosis he having had encephalographic studies and pneumo-encephalogram. The patient this date is competent according to VA regulations and not believed psychotic this date. He has been working as indicated above and intends to continue in school.

NEUROLOGICAL: Neurological examination of this patient was not requested and not found indicated and therefore not done.

DIAGNOSIS: 1. Paranoid state (history primarily), competent.

Chas B Huber MD
C. B. HUBER, M. D.
Neuropsychiatrist

STAGNER, Clyde Hurchell C-14 073 858

AREA CODE 813: 988-4131

COLLEGE OF ENGINEERING
OFFICE OF THE DEAN

March 14, 1969

Mr. Guy R. Nichols
Adjudication Officer
Veterans Administration
Regional Office
P. O. Box 1437
St. Petersburg, Florida 33731

Dear Mr. Nichols:

Re: Mr. Clyde H. Stagner
317 (21E)
C 14 073 858

This is to certify that the above referenced student has been accepted into the College of Engineering, Department of Energy Conversion at the University of South Florida.

Mr. Stagner must complete 99 quarter hours of work in the engineering field. Based on 15 quarter hours per semester this will take in excess of 6 quarters to complete.

I feel it is valid to say that the work Mr. Stagner has completed and is presently taking at the University is transferable to satisfy the basic studies and non-technical requirements of the College of Engineering. As a consequence there will be no substantial loss of credit associated with this change of major.

If I can furnish you further information or be of assistance, please do not hesitate to call on me.

Sincerely,

E. W. Kopp
E. W. Kopp
Dean

cc: Dr. L. A. Scott, Chairman
Department of Energy Conversion

Vet appeared in person 3-27-69. I questioned him about the 182 hours he had prior to enrollment at USF in Sept 1968 and the fact the school enrolled him in the "lower division". Vet was in service and continuously took "courses", most of which were Freshman & Soph subjects. Therefore there was a large percent not acceptable toward a degree. He said this would be true whether he worked toward a degree in Engineering or some other major. OK to ~~[illegible] Supv. [illegible]~~ authorize

Office of U. S. Senator Dennis DeConcini

1992 OCT 16 [illegible]

The Privacy Act of 1974 (P.L. 93-579) became fully effective on September 27, 1975. The purpose of the Act is to control the Federal Government's collection and dissemination of personal information about citizens. One of the provisions of the Act prohibits the Federal Government from revealing any information from any citizen's governmental records without the express permission of the person involved.

The Privacy Act does not authorize the disclosure of records to Members of Congress acting in their individual capacities or on behalf of their constituents, unless the individual to whom the record pertains has consented.

To assist you with your recent inquiry, I request that you complete and return to me the statement below.

I authorize Senator Dennis DeConcini or his staff to make inquiries on my behalf pertaining to the following matter: (Please give a brief description of your difficulties.)

On May 1, 1964 I was retired medically from the U.S. Army with 30% disability for paranoia, chronic, severe with a specific diagnosis of "suspiciousness" this retirement was pursuant to a applicable US Code. On 13 May 1992, while at the VA Medical Center at Tucson, I observed that the above diagnosis had been changed to schizophrenia Paranoid. This was a computer readout on top of my file and also on top of the medical refill list. On [illegible] 1992, while at the Tucson VA Medical Center I noted that the above diagnosis had been changed to psychosis. I have not been under psychiatric care at the Tucson VA Med Center for any of the above diagnoses. I request your assistance in restoring the diagnosis on all my VA records to paranoia, chronic, severe, with specific diagnosis of suspiciousness and require the VA Medical Center in Tucson to explain why the above changes in diagnosis occurred.

Signature: Clyde H Stagner Date: 16 Oct 1992 (CHS above, Oct 1992)

Name: (please print) CLYDE H STAGNER

Address: 8565 PEMBROOK DRIVE

City TUCSON State AZ Zip 85715

Telephones: Home: 2989192 Business: N/A

Social Security Number: 349-12-3030

Other File Number(s): (VA, CSC, OWCP, etc.) VA C14073858 US 36753278 WW# 02205[illegible]

A-2

DEPARTMENT OF HEALTH, EDUCATION, AND WELFARE
SOCIAL SECURITY ADMINISTRATION
BALTIMORE, MARYLAND 21241

REFER TO: IDI-613B
349-12-3030

July 18, 1978

BUREAU OF
DISABILITY INSURANCE

Veterans Administration
Regional Office
Attention: Mr. M. R. Woodall
Adjudication Officer
P.O. Box 1437
St. Petersburg, Florida 33731

Dear Mr. Woodall:

This is in reply to your request for medical information obtained in connection with the disability claim of Mr. Clyde H. Stanger.

Enclosed are copies of the medical reports, Alfred D. Koenig, M.D., dated September 20, 1976; Joseph A. Ezzo, M.D., dated September 5, 1975; and Bruce E. Parrish, M.D., various dates. This information is confidential. It is to be used only for the administration of your program. Federal law and regulations restrict its disclosure for any other purpose. Any inquiry concerning this evidence should be referred to us.

Other medical reports were submitted by the Veterans Administration Hospital, St. Petersburg, Florids. We assume that this information is available to you.

Sincerely yours,

Arthur F. Simermeyer
Assistant Bureau Director. Operations

Enclosures

DEPARTMENT OF VETERANS AFFAIRS
MEDICAL CENTER
TUCSON, AZ 85723

November 11, 1992

In Reply Refer To: 678/136
349-12-3030

Mr. Clyde H. Stagner
8565 Pembrook Drive
Tucson, AZ 85715

Dear Mr. Stagner:

This responds to your recent letter in which you expressed concerns over inconsistencies in your records relating to your diagnosis.

Let me begin by explaining that you have two sets of records within the Department of Veterans Affairs. One set, referred to as your Claims Folder, or C-File, resides at the VA Regional Office in Phoenix. This record contains medical documents from your active duty military service as well as all documents relating to adjudication of your service connected disabilities. The second set, maintained at the Tucson VA Medical Center, contains documents recording your medical treatment received from a VA Medical Center. Documentation in the two sets of records may contain different medical terms to describe a patient's condition. In your particular case, Mr. Stagner, using different terminology has no impact on your treatment, percentage of service connection or description of your condition. Psychosis is a broad general term that covers many mental disorders, including paranoia, schizophrenia and others. We have verified with staff at the Phoenix VA Regional Office that your official service connected condition for compensation purposes is listed a schizophrenia reaction, paranoid type. For treatment purposes, any of the terms you have listed are interchangeable.

I can understand the confusion the documentation may have caused you and am glad for the opportunity to clarify this matter for you.

Should you have further questions or concerns, please contact our Medical Administration staff at 792-1450, extension 6491.

Sincerely yours,

R.E. Lindsey, Jr.
Medical Center Director

Incl Pc

November 10, 1992

Sharon Chapman, Chief, Medical Information Svc.
VA Medical Center
Tucson, AZ 85723

Dear Ms. Chapman:

I would like my computer/medical records to reflect the change in diagnosis (return to original diagnosis) as stated in the attached documents.

I can be reached at 298-9192 if you have any questions.

Sincerely,

Clyde Stagner
8565 Pembrook Drive
Tucson, AZ 85715

cc: Bob Trinkhorn, VFW

Incl 4 b

DEPARTMENT OF VETERANS AFFAIRS
3225 N. CENTRAL AVENUE
PHOENIX, AZ 85012

February 10, 1993

In Reply Refer To: 345/273
C - 14 073 858

Mr. Clyde H. Stagner
8565 Pembrook Drive
Tucson, AZ 85715

The following information is furnished in reply to your inquiry of October 16, 1992 with Senator Deconcini's office. Please note the paragraphs checked below.

☐ 1. Action on your claim has been completed. You should receive a check within the next ________ days. If you do not, please contact us.

☐ 2. We need additional information to process your claim. Please submit the following document(s):

☐ 3. We have requested the following evidence or information from ____________________
____________________:

☐ a. Military records ☐ b. Hospital records ☐ c. ____________

When the documentation is received, we will take action on your claim.

☐ 4. A deduction of $__________ is being applied to an overpayment in the amount of $__________. The balance of overpayment as of ____________________ is $__________.

☐ 5. Your claim is now in the Rating Board for a decision. You will be notified of the determination in your case within approximately________ days.

[xx] 6. Enclosed is a copy of the latest rating decision on you dated 3/30/90. As you can see, you are rated 30% service connected for paranoid state, competent. Our computer system reflects a generic condition of psychosis for diagnostic code 9203. If your medical records at the VA Medical Center reflect other than paranoid state, competent or psychosis, then you should request, thru the medical center, that they be changed.

Sincerely yours,

Gerard K. Gessner
GERARD K. GESSNER
Veterans Services Officer(119)

Incl Va

cstampingr@dakotacom.net

From: "Johanna Eubank" <jeubank@azstarnet.com>
To: <cstamping@dakotacom.net>
Sent: Tuesday, January 13, 2009 12:18 PM
Subject: Permission to reprint article

Mr. Stagner,

You have permission to use the following article in your book. Please include all of the text, credit Tom Turner and the Arizona Daily Star and note that it ran in the Star Oct. 4, 1994.

Please let me know if you have any questions.

The article:

Soulful view of human nature; Movie captured Tucsonan's ordeal
By Tom Turner
Source: *THE ARIZONA DAILY STAR*
Tuesday,October 4, 1994
Edition: tue, Section: ACCENT, Page 1C

Clyde Stagner's fingers kneaded his lap gently, but his expression was stoic as he watched actress Jessica Lange writhe in the arms of another man, just as Stagner's wife did 32 years ago on an Alabama Army post.

On the Century Park Theater screen in front of him last week, actor Tommy Lee Jones wore the same look of stoicism, just before he carried Lange outside and dumped her in a swimming pool.

Stagner, 70, smiled then. Jones plays Stagner in the new film "Blue Sky." Lange plays his ex-wife, who is now dead. "Blue Sky" is not truly Stagner's life story. He was not a prominent whistle-blower on nuclear testing as the screen character is, but it's close enough to his life to draw on some buried emotions.

The screenplay was co-written by Stagner's daughter, Rama Laurie Stagner, a successful writer for television. This is her first movie script.

"In 1975, I wrote a manuscript on military events and a little on the married life," Stagner said. "It just sat on a shelf until the 1980s, when Rama said, 'You, know, Dad, I bet I could do something with this.' What she did basically was rewrite it from the perspective of her sister, Nickie, and herself."

On screen they are the Marshall family: Maj. Henry Marshall, his fantasy-driven wife, Carly, and their two daughters, Alex and Becky.

Actually, there were five Stagner children. And, while Carly engages in only one extramarital affair on screen, with her husband's commanding officer, the real Mrs. Stagner - Gloria - engaged many men at Fort McClellan, Ala. (Fort Matthews in the film), Stagner said.

"Jessica Lange is my first wife," Stagner said later. "She plays her to perfection." Lange never met Gloria. She died in 1982. But Lange spent a lot of time talking to Rama Stagner about her mother. Nor did Jones meet Stagner. His portrayal was drawn purely from the script.

"I am truly amazed with the way Tony Richardson took this story of real relationships and covered them with an allegorical veneer about the morality of nuclear testing," Stagner said.

Richardson, the film's director, died a year after shooting was completed.

Stagner joined the Army in 1943 and fought in World War II as an enlisted man. After the war, he was promised an appointment to West Point but dropped out of Amherst College after seven months and returned to his boyhood home in Joliet, Ill., where he worked in an arsenal. He enrolled in junior college and earned a commission in the Army Reserve.

Stagner met Gloria in Richmond, Va., and they were married in 1949. He received a Regular Army commission in 1951 and was assigned to Germany. By the late '50s, Stagner was assigned to Hawaii as commander of an armored personnel carrier.

He transferred to the Army Chemical Corps at Fort McClellan after his commander in Hawaii complained publicly about Gloria's behavior. That's where the story of "Blue Sky" begins.

There is another element in the "Blue Sky" story that skims close to Stagner's life. The Army forced Capt. Stagner (the movie "promoted" him) into hospitalization for mental illness, then discharged him for medical reasons without explanation, just as it did Maj. Marshall on the screen.

In the film, Marshall is institutionalized after he threatens to go public with the knowledge that two Nevada cowboys were inadvertently exposed to radiation in a nuclear test, known as the "Blue Sky Project."

"Actually, two cowboys were exposed to radiation in the Event Platte test in May 1962," Stagner said. "I was there, but I didn't see the two men and I have no idea what happened to them. In fact, many people were exposed in that burst. Later, in the Small Boy above-ground test, a group of Marines was exposed.

"I was there also, as radiation safety officer," Stagner said. "Back at McClellan, I had been teaching how to evaluate radiation effects from helicopters and fixed-wing aircraft, but I was not allowed to do that in Nevada. No one was observing the test sites from the air. No one was evaluating the downwind effects on civilians at all. I asked to be transferred back to McClellan, and I was."

Back in Alabama, agitation was increasing over the push for civil rights, seen by many Southerners - military included - as coming directly from John F. Kennedy's White House. Stagner says he was alarmed when a group of military officers at McClellan passed a resolution opposing the president's civil-rights stand.

"It was political, contrary to the Hatch Act, which forbids political activism in the military," Stagner says. "In my view, it was treasonous."

In August 1963, Stagner was ordered into an Army hospital for psychological evaluation. Early in 1964, he was discharged from the service.

"I was diagnosed as having schizophrenic paranoia with psychosis," he said. "I have never been treated or medicated for that since."

His military career behind him, Stagner packed up his family and moved them to Fresno, Calif. The Stagners were divorced a year later, in 1965.

He moved to Florida, where in 1968 he met and married Virginia Elizabeth, a widow with six children of her own, five of whom Stagner adopted. Later, his two sons by Gloria also joined them. His daughters stayed with their mother. Still later, when his youngest biological daughter died, leaving a 7-year-old son, Stagner and his new family raised him, too.

To support the expansive brood, Stagner worked in radiation detection and nuclear planning for the Pinellas County, Fla., Health Department, the Florida Power Corp. and the city of St. Petersburg. Along the way he earned a degree in engineering. He retired in 1974.

In 1980, the Stagners moved to Tucson because of a daughter's asthma. "We've never been sorry," he said.

"One of the greatest thrills was when my dad was hired as a consultant ("Nuclear Effects Advisor," it says in the screen credits) when the film went into production," Rama Stagner said in a studio news release.

"The film closed a breach in my family created when we all shut down to avoid looking at the painful truth," Rama said.

"One thing is sure. Gloria was never a heroine," Stagner said. "That part is pure fiction, but it makes a terrific movie."

BLUE SKY

Cast

Carly Marshall: Jessica Lange
Hank Marshall: Tommy Lee Jones
Vince Johnson: Powers Boothe
Vera Johnson: Carrie Snodgress
Alex Marshall: Amy Locane
Glenn Johnson: Chris O'Donnell
Ray Stevens: Mitchell Ryan
Colonel Mike Anwalt: Dale Dye
Ned Owens: Tim Scott
Lydia: Annie Ross
Becky Marshall: Anna Klemp

and in Order of Appearance

Helicopter Pilot: Anthony Rene Jones
Soldier on Island: Jay H. Seidl
Soldier #1: David Bradford
NATO Soldier: Matt Battaglia
NATO Officers: Rene Rokk, Fred Scasso, Victor Iemolo, Bronson Page, Raphael Rey Gomez, Samy G. Buaso
Adjutant: John J. Fedak
Lt. Colonel Jennings: Michael McClendon
Salesladies: Harriet Courtney Sumner, Shannon Laramore
Administrative 1st Sergeant: Ray Sergeant
Lt. Colonel George Land: Merlin Marston
Officers' Wives: Yvette Smedley, Phyllis Timbes, Libby Whittemore, Clarinda Ross, Donna Biscoe
Band Leader: Billy Lawson
Soldier at Bar: Joseph Wilkins
Attention Sergeant: Carl C. Morgan III
General Derrick: Dion Anderson
Jimmy: Richard Jones
Piano Player: Art Wheeler
Nurse: Sharlene Ross
Stockade Guard: David Lee Lane
Stockade MP: Ed Lee Corbin
Doctor Vankay: Gary Bullock
Dottie Owens: Angela Paton
Reporters: Babs George, Rod Masterson, Sean McGraw
Newscaster: David Dwyer
Engineer: Geoff McKnight
Desk Clerk: Whitt Brantley
Stunts performed by: Don Pike, Diane Peterson, Gary Pike, Joni Avery, Eric Norris, Greg Gault

84

Orion Pictures presents
A Robert H. Solo Production
A Tony Richardson Film

Directed by: Tony Richardson
Produced by: Robert H. Solo
Story by: Rama Laurie Stagner
Screenplay by: Rama Laurie Stagner, Arlene Sarner & Jerry Leichling
Co-Producer: Lynn Arost
Supervising Producer: John G. Wilson
Director of Photography: Steve Yaconelli
Film Editor: Robert K. Lambert, A.C.E.
Production Designer: Timian Alsaker
Costume Designer: Jane Robinson
Music by: Jack Nitzsche
Casting by: Lynn Stalmaster
Associate Producer: Rama Laurie Stagner
Unit Production Manager: John G. Wilson
First Assistant Director: Thomas J. Mack
Second Assistant Director: David Kelley
Art Director: Gary John Constable
Set Decorator: Leslie Rollins
Lead Man: Tal C. Schneider
Property Master: Sean Mannion
Assistant Props: Thomas Gleason
Camera Operator: Candy Gonzales
Helicopter Camera Operator: Roger Lee Smith
First Assistant Camera: Terence Nightingall
Second Assistant Camera: Daniel Dayton, Joe Ponticelle, Bruce Kuehn
Production Sound Mixers: Jacob Goldstein, Susumu Tokunow
Boom Operators: Joel Racheff, Kathleen Pud Cusack
Second Unit Director: Robert K. Lambert
Production Associate: Michael Casey
Script Supervisor: Kate Lewis
Second 2nd Assistant Director: Stefanie A. Moore
Production Coordinator: Anna Zappia
Assistant to Tony Richardson: David Bradford
Key Grip: Frank Keever
Best Boy Grip: Victor Shelehov
Dolly Grip: Scott Leftridge
Grips: Doug Cowden, Michael Alexonis, Sean Slattery
Gaffer: Ross Maehl
Best Boy Electric: Roger Sassen
Lighting Technicians: Eric Maehl, Tim Magaraci, Carl Johnson, Anthony Avilsden
Assistant Editors: Mike Solinger, Scott Taylor
Post Production Supervisor: Sara Romilly & Michael J. Hacker
Supervising Sound Editor: Bruce Richardson

Supervising ADR Editor: Thomas Whiting
Music Editor: Richard Whitfield
Sound Effect Editors: Albert Gasser, Constance A. Kazmer, Gary Wright, Pamela Bentkowski, Richard King, Marguerite Costin
ADR Editor: Denise Whiting Gontz
Assistant Sound Editor: David Lee Hagberg
Assistant ADR Editors: Stephanie Krivacek, Linda Yeaney
Apprentice Sound Editor: Eric Orlow
Wardrobe Stylist for Ms. Lange: Joanne Lam
Wardrobe Supervisor: P. Kay Morris
Women's Costumer: Shari Gray
Men's Costumer: Tony Velasco
Costumer: Antoinette Squeo
Wardrobe Assistant: Helen R. Monaghan
Makeup Artist for Ms. Lange: Dorothy Pearl
Makeup Artist: Bob Arrollo
Assistant Makeup & Hair: Teresa Austin
Hair Stylist for Ms. Lange: Lyndell Quiyou
Key Hairstylist: Cydney Cornell
Assistant Hair: Star Orr
Stunt Coordinator: Don Pike
Special Effects: Cliff Wenger, Mack Chapman
Choreographed by: Greg Rosatti
Extras Casting: Tonya Suzanne
Publicist: Lauren Hyman
Still Photographers: Abram S. Perlstein, Cliff Lipson
Public Relations (Alabama): Erskine C. Minor
Teacher: Denise M. Smith
Production Auditor: Cynthia Quan
Assistant Auditor: Gail Foreman
Post-Production Auditor: Marlla Meggett
Disbursing Agent: Shauna L. Kroen
Assistant Production Coordinator: Damian Ganczewski
Assistant to Robert Solo: Randi Berez
Assistant to Lynn Arost: Nicholas Vlorst
Assistant to John G. Wilson: Jack Teetor
Set Dressers: Matt A. Marich, Kimberly Lannaghan, Lloyd R. Whittaker, Robin Solo
Set Dressing Assistants (Florida): Suzanne Dimmler, Richard Dimmler
Shopper: Alice Walker Persons
Transportation Coordinator: John P. McAuliffe
Transportation Captain: Robert Voss
Picture Cars: James Rutledge
Locations Manager: James Morris
Locations (Alabama): William Brett Haas
Locations (Florida): Steve Franklin
Locations (Texas): Michael Charske
Construction Coordinator: Star Fields
Lead Carpenter: G. Ron Wright, Jr.
Draftsman: Robert L. Berry
Lead Scenic Artist: Joel Griffith
Scenic Artist: Geoi Lynn Welch
Stand By Scenic Artist: Karen Anne Gower
Foreman: James Mack Blair
Carpenters: Peter G. Gulick, Vincent D. Marra, Tony Valdes, Mark Peltier, Brian McKinsey
Military Advisor: James P. Monaghan
Nuclear Effects Advisor: Clyde H. Stagner
Marine Coordinator: Frances Knight
Aviation Coordinator: Charlie R. Hillard
Helicopter Pilots: Robert Smith, Ben Oliver, Jim Wikert, Harry Haus, Eugene Nock, John Hayden, Paul Barth
Production Assistants: Robert E. Schick, Susan Rubin, Jennifer E. Lumpkin
Post Production Assistant: Daniel Steinberg
Stand-Ins: Patti Miller, Richard Russell
First Aid: Linda B. Sedlak, Louise Shaw
Caterer: Jose Ruben Quintero
Catering Assistant: P. Jean Wilson
Craft Services: Vickie Reigle
Drivers: George Yarbrough, Genny Elliott, Joe Pat Price, Larry Shephard, Marshall Hovies
Re-Recorded at: Warner Hollywood Studios
Re-Recording Mixers: Robert J. Litt, Greg P. Russell, C.A.S., Elliot Tyson
Recordists: Jack Keller, David Behle
ADR Mixer: Thomas J. O'Connell
ADR Recordist: Rick Canelli
Foley Recorded at: Todd A-O/Glen Glenn Sound
Mixer: Dean Drabin
Foley Artists: Robin Harlan, Sarah Jacobs
Music Score Produced by: Michael Hoenig
Electronic Keyboards Performed by: Bradford Ellis
Featured Solo Performance by: David Lindley
Scoring Engineer: Pamela Neal
Music Consultant: Sharal Churchill
Negative Cutting: D. Bassett & Associates, Inc.
Color Timer: Michael Milliken
Titles & Opticals by: CFI EFX
Insurance: Albert G. Ruben & Co., Inc.
Completion Bond: The Completion Bond Co., Inc.
Payroll Service: Disc Payroll Services
Music Supervision by: Jackie Krost

"(BABY) YOU'VE GOT WHAT IT TAKES"
Written by Clyde Otis, Murray Stein
Performed by Brook Benton & Dinah Washington
Courtesy of PolyGram Special Productions
a division of PolyGram Group Distribution, Inc.

"MALAGUENA"
Written by Ernesto Lecuona
Performed by The Billy Lawson Band

"YOUNG MIND"
Written by Johnny Meyers
Performed by Johnny Meyers & Amos Milburn
Courtesy of Ace Records, Inc.

COMPENSATION AND PENSION EXAM INQUIRY

```
         Name: STAGNER,CLYDE H
          SSN: 349123030
     C-Number: 14073858
          DOB: JUL 27,1924
      Address: 8565 PEMBROOK DRIVE

City,State,Zip+4: TUCSON, ARIZONA 85715
       Res Phone: 520-298-9192
       Bus Phone: 000-000-0000
Entered active service: FEB 26,1949
Released active service: MAY 1,1964
```

>>> Future C&P Appointments <<<

Requested exams currently on file:
GENERAL MEDICAL EXAMINATION
Requested on DEC 10,2002@13:23:51 by SOUTHERN ARIZONA HCS - Open

---

This request was initiated on DEC 10,2002 at 13:23:51
Requester: HAZE,WILLIAM J
Requesting Regional Office: SOUTHERN ARIZONA HCS

Exams on this request:
GENERAL MEDICAL

** Status of request:
New

RATED DISABILITIES:
PSYCHOSIS, SCHIZ PARA 30 %
Service-Connected? Yes DX Code: 9203
GOUT 20 %
Service-Connected? Yes DX Code: 5017
SINUSITIS,MAXILLARY,CHRONIC 10 %
Service-Connected? Yes DX Code: 6513
BRONCHITIS,CHRONIC 10 %
Service-Connected? Yes DX Code: 6600
CIRRHOSIS OF LIVER 0 %
Service-Connected? Yes DX Code: 7312
HEMORRHOIDS 0 %
Service-Connected? Yes DX Code: 7336

Other Disabilities: SEE COMMENTS

General Remarks:
-GENERAL MEDICAL EXAM NEEDED FOR:
1. BACK CONDITION-ARTHRITIS
-PLEASE ADDRESS DELUCA REQUIREMENTS.

8565 Pembrook Drive
Tucson
Az 85715

31 July 2004

T0:Dr. James and Mrs. Jeannie Callan
Occasion:Family Reunion

Dear Jim And Jeannie,

The following narrative may be of interest to you.

In May,1962,I asked to be,and was, replaced as the Department of Defense(DOD) Radiological Safety Officer at the Nevada Test Site. My request for helicopters to radiolgically survey the off site fallout from the forthcoming suface Event Little Boy had been denied. Previously,the US Public Health Sevice fixed wing aircraft tried to warn two cowboys(as in Blue Sky) out of the fallout from the DOD Event Plattee(April,1962) by waggling its wings.

Cica Oct,1962,I attended a Sojourner`s private meeting in the Fort McClellan,Ala, Officer`s Club. Sojourners are are Masons who are officers,past,or present,who take an oath to defend the United States against all enemies. At this meeting,Col Dozier,Commanding Officer,100th Chemical Group,introduced a resolution to oppose President John F Kennedy(for whom I did not vote),cited a list of reasons therefore,and proposed joining with other organizations(not cited) to oppose the President. The word "POLITICAL" was not included during the reading of this resolution,or cited in any discussion thereafter. Some of the reasons cited(I do not recall all of them) are included in the following:

1. Removing air cover from the Bay of Pigs Invasion of Cuba

2.Failure to invade Cuba militarily.

3.Removing US missiles from Turkey to appease Kruschev in the removal of Russian missles from Cuba.

4.Treaty ban with Russia on above ground nuclear tests. Little Boy,cited supra,was the last scheduled US nuclear surface test.

After being recognized,I arose and objected to the proposed resolution(See the attached polygraph for my reasons). Sitting on my left,reserve CWO Woodruff(now deceased) asked me,"Aren`t you opposed to a leftist dictator taking over this country?" My response was,"I am against a dictator taking over this country,whether from the left or the right". The meeting adjourned. This is the same "Woody" Woodruff who assisted you,Jim, in the Anniston,Ala,De Molay-I vividly recall your beautiful Mother`s Day Flower Talk in 1961.

The morning after the meeting,while driving our next door neighbor,Maj. Amos Johnson(now deceased),to his office,I asked him,"What are you people trying to do?". His answer,"Save the country from where it`s headed." Maj. Johnson never answered the question. Circa this time,the integration of "Ole Miss" was a national event-Fort McClellan had sent troops to its neighboring Mississippi.

5.President Kennedy sent troops to "Ole Miss" to force its integration.

Several weeks later,I was ordered to report to the Conference Room of the Chemical Corps School where Col. Laverne Parks,Commandant of the school:Col. Wallace,Commanding Officer,Hospital Commander; and Maj. Amos Johnson awaited me.. A new,and different, Sojourner Resolution was handed me with pen I was ordered, "Make any changes you wish." After my reading,it was handed back without change and I was dismissed from "my military career death chamber."

Approximately a month later in the Officer`s Club,Col Palmer,recently retired as Commanding Officer of the Chemical Corp`s Pine Bluff Arsenal, in Arkansas engaged me in conversation. He apprised me that his Sojourners Chapter in Pine Bluff had received the same resolution and he had it tabled accoding tp parliamentary protocol. This knowledge reared the spectre that all other approximately 250 Sojourners Chapters had also received the same resolution. Someone,somewhere,had decided President Kennedy was an enemy of the United States. Sojourner`s Headquarters were,and still are,in Alexandria,Va.

In October,1963,Col Parks ordered me, in writing, to report to the Commanding Officer,Noble Army Hospital,Fort McClellan,Ala for psychiatric evaluation(which I refused to do voluntarily). After reporting,Iwas restricted to the hospital. Days later,I was tranquillized , air freighted to the US Army Valley Forge General Hospital, and locked up in a psychiatric ward. During the tenure in Noble Army Hospital,and my winter at Valley Forge,my experiences with the Sojourners was never divulged. From a lock ward,Iwatched the assination of President Kennedy. By coincidence? By design?

Incl 26 page 1

Controlled fear returned reminiscent of the zig-zagging unescorted troop ship ridden to New Guinea in World War II. Maintaining my silence,I was medically retired from the US Army on 1 May 1964 with 30% pemanent disability for Paranoia;specific diagnosis:Suspiciousness. My military medical records were sent to the Veterans Administration Regional Office,Chicago,Ill, where my diagnosis was administratively(without medical examination) changed to Paranoid Schizophrenic. My efforts to correct this with the VA have failed,and as of 2004,the VA Inspector General has not responded to this issue.

Since the assination,I have seen a copy of a National Security Action Memorandum,signed by President Kennedy within thirty days prior to his death,in which 1000 troops were ordered out of Viet Nam by 1 Jan,1964.

6. President Kennedy was going to withdraw the US Forces from Viet Nam

President Johnson countermanded the order,and with the Gulf of Tonkin Resolution from Congress went on to full scale military conflict.

In 1976,with the assistance of Virginia,my loving wife,an attempt was made to novelize the above experiences which resulted in a manuscript entitled,"The Muted Bugle". Several attempts at movie scripts failed. In 1989,Rama Laurie,using some of the military experiences,presented through the eyes of two daughters(essentially Nicki and Laurie),wrote her first movie script which was the movie "Blue Sky".

Note: In Jan,1965, Rama Laurie visited Col Dozier and his family at the Presidio in San Francisco for a weekend with his daughter.

Circa 1977,a first page article in the Sojourner's magazine contained a US Army Major's damning berating of President Kennedy's denying air cover for the Bay of Pigs. What are the "politics" of his berating a deceased president?

There are Constitutional means for the removal of a US president,ie President Nixon in the early 1970's. The Constitutrion of the United States is the umbrella under which we move,think, and live. To defend it ,is to protect our self survival

My memories of Masonry being used as described herein vis-a-vis the charitable and benificent efforts of the majority of Masons worldwide will remain my nemesis.

God Bless You,Love You Both

Clyde

Member,Bredablick Lodge No. 0880,F&AM,1951
Member,Scottish Rite of Freemasons,SJ,USA,1955
Valley of American Military
Orient of NATO Bases
Noble,Sabbar Shrine
A.A.O.N.M.S. of Tucson,AZ 1982
Nonmember,National Sojourners
member,Heroes of 76 NYPE 1951

cc Nicki,daughter,and husband Jocko Marcellino
Rama Laurie Stagner,daughter, and husband Dan Witt
Bonnie, daughter, and husband David Lord
Mark.son, and wife Kim
Cindi,daughter,and husband David Stevens
Joseph,son,and wife Denise
Ralph Scott,son,and wife Shari
Michael Stagner,son
Virginia,daughter,and husband Roger Huston
Carolyn Alton.daughter

Incl 26 Page

SOUTHWEST POLYGRAPH SERVICES, INC.

615 N. SWAN
TUCSON, AZ. 85711
(602) 326-4756
FAX #(602) 327-0753

FILE NO:	92-0918A
SUBJECT:	CLYDE HURCHEL STAGNER
CLIENT:	CLYDE HURCHEL STAGNER
TYPE OF TEST:	SPECIFIC
DATE OF TEST:	6/12/92
ATTENTION:	CLYDE HURCHEL STAGNER

On June 12, 1992 Clyde Hurchel Stagner came to the offices of Southwest Polygraph Services for the purpose of examination by polygraph technique to determine whether or not between August and November of 1962 he attended a Chapter Meeting of the National Sojourners wherein a resolution was proposed that was treasonous in nature in the opinion of subject.

During the pre-test interview, subject related that he was an officer in the United States Army at the time. Further, that the National Sojourners consists of officers from all branches of the United States Military; that during this particular Chapter Meeting one Colonel Dozier, United States Army (no further description), allegedly read a Resolution to the various Military Officers present at that meeting. Those that he could recall were Chief Warrant Officer Woody Woodruff, Major Amos Johnson, et al. Subject related Colonel Dozier proposed a Resolution to the membership opposing then President of the United States John Fitzgerald Kennedy, additionally, proposing that the National Sojourners affiliate themselves politically with civilian political actions.

Subject related that pursuant to his perception, his military oath, and the Hatch act, such a Resolution was in his opinion, treasonous, in violation of his military oath and the constitution of the United States.

Further that he orally objected pursuant to procedure to that Resolution, stating his reasoning.

Continuing, subject related some time after that meeting, within weeks or several months, he conversed with a Colonel John Palmer, United States Army, who belonged to another chapter of the National Sojourners. Further, Colonel Palmer allegedly informed subject that a similar, or the same, Resolution was proposed to his chapter meeting and subsequently failed after objection.

Balance of the pre-test interview was favorable.

The following relevant questions were asked and subject's answers recording.

1. *During 1962, did you make up a story about Colonel Dozier proposing a resolution at your National Sojourner's chapter, opposing President Kennedy.*
   ANS: NO.

2. *Did you make up a story about that President Kennedy proposed resolution being treasonous in your opinion?*
   ANS: NO.

3. *Did you make up a story about orally objecting to that 1962 President Kennedy resolution because it was treasonous in your opinion?*
   ANS: NO.

4. *During latter 1962, did you make up a story about Colonel John Palmer telling you a similar treasonous Kennedy resolution had been proposed at his chapter of the National Sojourners?*
   ANS: NO.

After careful evaluation and numerical analysis it is the opinion of this examiner that subject's responses to the above relevant questions asked and answers recorded were truthful.

The Reid MGQT Technique was utilized during the examination wherein three polygrams were recorded, duly signed by the subject, and made a permanent part of this file along with other related data.

James W. Moffett

JWM:ap

REPLY TO REQUEST FOR ORGANIZATIONAL RECORDS (MEDICAL) | STAGNER, CLYDE H.

SPONSOR'S NAME	SPONSOR'S SERVICE/SOCIAL SECURITY NUMBER	BRANCH OF SERVICE
--	--	--

☒ A search of our medical record holdings was made based on the information you provided. The results of our search are shown below. The following is key to the abbreviations used: C/R- Clinical (Inpatient) Records; O/P-Outpatient Treatment Records; M/H Mental Hygiene Consultation Files; and D/R-Dental Records.

Type of Record	Treatment Facility	Dates	Results of Search
C/R	VALLY FORGE	1964	Note 4
N/A			N/A
N/A			N/A
N/A			N/A

Results of Search

Note 1. The requested copies are enclosed. We regret that some of the copies may be of poor quality; however they are the best copies obtainable.

Note 2. A record for the patient named above was not on file. If you are able to obtain additional information from the treatment facility regarding the retirement of the record, please resubmit your request and we will make a further search. The following information is needed from the treatment facility; accession number, box number, and location number.

Note 3. These records have not yet been retired to this Center. We suggest you contact the treatment facility at the address shown below to obtain the requested record.

Note 4. The requested record has been lent to the Department of Veterans Affairs (VA). Please phone the VA at 1-800-827-1000 for help in obtaining this record, and provide your VA Claim Number: C-

Note 5. The requested record has been lent to the office shown below and may be obtained by writing directly to that facility at the address shown.

☐ Clinical records and mental hygiene consultation files are retired by the treatment facility and filed in this Center according to the facility, status of patient, and month/year of EACH hospitalization or consultation. Outpatient treatment records and dental records normally follow the patient when a change of station occurs; therefore, they are retired by the last LAST treatment facility and filed in this Center according to the facility, status of the patient and month/year of LAST treatment. Please complete the enclosed NA Form 13042, Request for Information Needed to Locate Medical Records, and resubmit it to this Center for further search.

☐ The Privacy Act of 1974 does not permit the release of a social security number or other personal information to the public without the authorization of the veteran concerned; therefore, we have deleted personal identifying data relating to other persons.

☐ The Department of Defense Privacy Program, 32 CFR310.a30(f), allows for the disclosure of medical records to the individual to whom they pertain. A portion of the requested medical records, however, contains information which can be interpreted and explained properly only by a physician. If you wish us to send copies to a designated physician, please provide us with the name and address of that physician. The request MUST INCLUDE the written consent (signature) of the person whose records are involved, authorizing the release of the records to the designated physician.

☒ VA Regional Office
2030 W. Taylor St.
Chicago, Ill.

CLYDE STAGNER
N/A
8565 PEMBROOK DRIVE
TUCSON, AZ 85715

Jan. 9, 2004
Date

Naomi Smotherman
Prepared by

☐ Operations Branch ☒ Records Retrieval Branch
☐ Reference Services Branch

NATIONAL PERSONNEL RECORDS CENTER

☐ Civilian Personnel Records
111 Winnebago Street
St. Louis, MO 63118-4199

☒ Military Personnel Records
9700 Page Avenue
St. Louis, MO 63132-5100

NATIONAL PERSONNEL RECORDS ADMINISTRATION NA FORM 13151 (REV. 02-02)

8565 Pembrook Drive
Tucson
Az 85715

April 24, 2004

VA Inspector General
PO Box 50410
Wash,DC 20091

RE:VA Diagnostic Coding
C1407385

Dear Inspector General

Your attention is respectfully invited to 38 CFR-Chapter I-Part 4,physchotic disorders. Documents cited herein are contained in Va Regional Office(Phoenix,Az)files.

Chronologically:

1. On 28 Feb 64,my Medical Board Proceedings,US Army Valley Forge General Hospital,Par,1.,listed a disability of "3030 Paranoid reaction * * * Marked (VA Code No. 9208)" .(Incl 1).

2. Subsequently,on 19 May 64,my US Army Physical Evaluation Board Proceedings listed"Paranoid reaction,Chronic, Definite, 9208".(Incl 2):

NOTE:VA Diagnostic Code 9208 is defined as Paranoid reaction(specify). The US Army specified suspiciousness.

3.After my military retirement on 1 May 64,a VA disability rating decision,based only on my military health records received,cites a VA Diagnostic Code of 9203 but defined as "Paranoid Reaction,Chronic,Competent". (Incl 3)

NOTE:VA Diagnostic Code9203,38CFR,is defined as"SCHIZOPHRENIC REACTION,PARANOID TYPE"

The undersigned believes an administrative error occurred in transposing the disability code from the US Army to the VA. Attempts to rectify the error have been unsuccessful(Incl 4a,4b,4c,and 4d) and the stigmatization arbritarily continues-from paranoid suspisciousness to paranoid schizophrenic.

The undersigned requests your assistance in correcting this degrading situation.

Sincerely,

Clyde H. Stagner
SSN 349123030
Tel :520 2989192

CHAPTER 4

REFLECTIONS

On an October morning in 2008, Stagner viewed the sun slowly rolling up and through Reddington Pass as its precursors shaded the west ern sky from dark to light. The Santa Catalina Mountains above Tucson came into ragged dominance. The id of the United States was about to change into facet reflections of different shades and hues, "Obama will be the next president of the United States". Past experiences in the U.S. Army raised questions in his mind concerning a repetitive Sojourner Resolution. Stagner chose to record those experiences and references in writing with documentation as the media for expressing his concern with due diligence, *"he, who asserts the following to be racist, is the racist".*

In 1949,Stagner`s friend, 2d Lt. Gale Lyman Larson, was his best man, and in1950, Stagner was his best man. Gale, a young Mason, was respected as a brother by other young officers. In 1951, Stagner asked Gale how he could possibly become a Mason, *"the Masonic oyster suppers during the great depression, in the old Channahon wooden townhall, were warm with their friendliness and those big oysters in a bowl of warm milk".* The asking, at that time, resulted in Stagner becoming a Mason in Stuyvesant Lodge in New York City. Stagner was impressed with the lodge members who were individualistically friendly, courteous, and helpful. Upon completion of his 3d degree, he was a master Mason and addressed by others members as, "Brother". To become a Mason, a belief in God was necessary with a respect for all religions that likewise believed in a single God entity. The discussion of religion or politics in a Masonic Lodge was forbidden, *"if only the northern and southern Irish and the Hindu/Muslims did likewise".*

The Masonic lodges in a given state, N.Y. in this case , all belonged to, and were under the jurisdiction of the Grand Lodge of that state. A master Mason was eligible to join one, or all, of the other Masonic entities under their respective, separate jurisdictions provided the jurisdictions recognized each other which involved "Blue Lodge" membership criteria common to all. Stagner enjoyed watching the varied ethnic people during the nickel subway rides to Manhattan from Brooklyn and return , " *a 2d Lieutenant on cavalry horse was synonymous with the military, but riding a subway in New York City".*

Stagner then joined the National Sojourners located at the New York Port of Embarkation in Brooklyn . Their meetings were held in historic Fort Hamilton where a ragged Stagner was allowed to cross the river and become a Hero of 76, *"once a hero ,always a hero".* The National Sojourners was composed of Chapters under the national jurisdiction of the National Sojourners, Inc. located in Alexandria ,Virginia. Membership eligibility required being a master Mason and an officer, past or present, of the military forces of the United States. Chapters were existent at many military installations in the United States and overseas where master Masons, at great distances from their Blue Lodges, met for fellowship. They were sworn to

defend the United States of America against all enemies whomsoever, *"although an enemy in your face is readily identifiable, those at a distance in some one else`s eye is another matter"*. Most Chapters had an appendant Encampment of Heroes of 76 where brave Sojourners were allowed to enter. The National Sojourners ,Inc.in Alexandria,Va. had an appendent National Encampment of Heroes of 76.

After attending the Infantry School in 1952,*"temporay duty of less than six months and one day left the family in Richmond"*. After graduation, assignment in 1952,to the 43d Infantry Division in Germany *"another five months without family while awaiting dependant housing"*. Leading an Infantry Company on a ground tour over most of southern Germany limited Stagner`s attendance at the Stuttgart Chapter of National Sojourners, *"that spring Saturday night, while on a command post exercise on the Nuremburg plain, when the four company commanders met at a German Gausthouse in the middle of nowhere, the drivers took turns guarding the jeeps, German beer leaving foam rings on the inside of the mugs, singing Duetches Uber Alles with the muscular farmers and their well endowed wives, being given beds to sleep upon and being awakened at 4AM to continue our duties, that was a night forever engraved. In 1952,only one in four Germans liked us, in 1955, three of four liked us"*.

In early 1955, Stagner attended Masonic Lodge meetings in the Stuttgart Bahnhof with the Mercedes Benz emblem at its peak. Although the Germans were forbidden to have secret meetings, on several occasions the Germans had to exit the lodge room before the Americans could enter.

After Germany received its sovereignty, Stagner, in the summer of 1955, traveled to Frankfurt, Germany, on a Friday and returned to Stuttgart the following Sunday evening as a 32d degree Mason and a member of Seneca Consistory #53,Valley of Main, Germany. His Masonic passport was in German; from the around his neck his neck hung a large black iron cross held by a ribbon striped with the German National colors of black, red, and gold..

By some unknown protocol, Stagner`s consistory was transferred from German jurisdiction to the Orient of California, Southern Jurisdiction of the Scottish Orient of NATO Bases, Southern Jurisdiction of the U.S. After Germany regained , Masonic Blue Lodge creation activity was at a frenzy in the American Zone of Germany . Stagner was a charter member in the start up of Hiram Lodge # 819 and Solomon Lodge # 822 including occupying the office of junior warden. Within a month, some one in the United States decided that a Mason could only belong to one Masonic lodge at a time: resignations (demits) from the lodges under German Jurisdiction were immediately submitted and accepted.

Sojourner members come from Blue Lodges; Blue Lodges plus Scottish Rite, Northern or Southern Jurisdiction; Blue Lodges plus York Rite; or any combination thereof. Members of Blue Lodges came from states, *"both*

***mental and locale"*, of varied social and political attributes which seldom became involved in day to day Military or social activities unless specifically mentioned, *"like the officer in Stuttgart in 1952 who loudly articulated on the number of KKK members who were senators and representatives in the U.S. Congress"*. Of relative significance is the Scottish Rite Creed , "Human progress is our cause, liberty of thought our supreme wish, freedom of conscience our mission and the guarantee of equal rights to all people everywhere our ultimate goal, *"and so these reflections continue"*. The Scottish Rite confers the 4th through the 32d degrees. Charity was always advocated within all Masonic entities and Activities, *"and obedience to Masonic protocol by ritual and title"*.**

Research, into the Scottish Rite, brought forth several items for consideration, *"shall Masonry hide, deny, or swerve from the truth by digression"* :

1. Albert Pike, a Mason and Confederate general was convicted of treason against the United States of America: his remains were in an alcove of the House of the Temple, Southern Juridsdiction, Wash, D.C., according to Wikipedia, the Free Encyclopedia.

2. The preface to the 1950 edition of Pike`s, "Morals and Dogma" include the following, "Everyone is entirely free to reject and dissent from whatsoever herein may seem to be untrue or unsound," according to Wikipedia , the Free Encyclopedia.

3. A copy of, " Morals and Dogma", was given to every new member of the Southern Jurisdiction until 1974 according to Wikipedia, the Free Encyclopedia.

4. His (Pikes) racism was nothing to be proud of according to the Grand Lodge of British Columbia.

5. There was cross membership between the KKK and Masonic Lodges according to John R. Snyder in the, "On the Level," Masonic Website and Newsletter.

6. On Feb. 1,1993, C. Fred Kleinknett, Sovereign Grand Commander of Freemasons Southern Jurisdiction of the United States asserted that the post-Civil War KKK was not a very bad organization, according to Schilla Institute, Fidelity Magazine.

According to Wikipedia, the Free Encyclopedia, the book, "Morals and Dogma," was never used in the Scottish Rite, Northern Jurisdiction, located in Lexington , Massachusetts, *"the German Jurisdiction did not issue, "Morals and Dogma", when the Seneca Consistory was joined in 1955"*.

The York Rite, like the Scottish Rite, conferred Masonic degrees beyond the 3d degree of the Blue Lodge. Membership in the Knights Templar and Order of Malta degrees required an invitation. The top degrees of the York Rite required an oath to Christianity and trilogy, *"is the taking of a Christian oath in a Masonic Jurisdiction the antitheses of the deist commitment made in the Blue Lodge, can the deist and Christian oaths be defined in interchangeable equity without redefining definitions , would those who willingly swear to*

defend the Christain faith also defend the Muslim faith, if such is the truth it could be included in the oath. the phrase, "defend the Christain faith," so prolifically used in the existence justification of multiple entities , resembles the snakes of Medusa".

Years of military experience included recollections of various relationships among army officers. Junior officers followed the orders of superior officers because of oaths, loyalty derived from that which satisfied their needs, or due to possible retribution in courts martial for failure to obey a lawful order. Only lawyers expert in military law were capable of defining an unlawful order except those such as, "march your men over that cliff". Going to a staff judge advocate(army lawyer) for clarification of a superior officer's order was tantamount to resignation in peacetime or the frontlines in wartime., *"although no orders were considered unlawful, the 2D Battalion Executive Officer, Maj.Winston's order to paint the troop's Sheridan Kaserne German Barracks without authorizing a requisition,or supplying the paint , was considered borderline".* There were no memories of a junior officer successfully challenging a superior officer's orders. Junior officers were followers, although some found coat tails to ride on , *"2d lieutenants were referred to as shave tails".*

Military intelligence officers assigned to installation and lower echelon unit staffs were the examples of inaction, *"except the National Guard S2 Captain, 2d Battalion, who came into Co C's Orderly Room and took its typewriter claiming it belonged back in New England; he had introduced the Battalion Commander to a beautiful, blond, available German fraulein"..* Receipt of information. analysis, and distribution of refined evaluated information was their recipe for functionality. In the Infantry, patrols and reconnaissance were sent out to observe and report. At higher echelons aerial photography, electromagnetic communication monitoring , and covert or overt human spies provided information for the intelligence officer behind the desk, *"several high ranking U.S. intelligence officers saved Japanese and German officers from war crimes trials in exchange for their espionage services, sleeping with the enemy who killed our own by torture".*Active operation were primarily a function of Special Operations or contractors. The CIA, in some cases, used the military for interrogations, *" military actions were under the Manual for Courts Martial which was a Presidential Executive Order which negated civil jurisdiction".*

Retired reserve army officers were only subject to courts martial when receiving medical treatment in a military hospital. Retired regular army officers were subject to courts martial until death with restrictions concerning post military employment, restrictions concerning criticism of designated political office holders, other official orders such as prohibited industrial contacts, and the many other restrictions and controls of the courts martial manual were applicable, *"some of these restrictions were*

residuals from the Indian Wars era, why were reserve officers now exempt from these restrictions".

No women or black U.S. Army officers were observed in attendance at any Masonic meeting on military post, camp ,station, or installation which Stagner attended, "*commanding the 39th Transportation Truck Company`s 1954 integration in Germany was a remembrance of white Noncommissioned Officers leaving the unit because the black First Sergeant was retained; Ist Sgt Brinson was a loyal, dependable, effective man; no complaints were ever received concerning the unit` s transport of the 7th Corps Headquarters within Germany."*

Sojourners members of other social, fraternal, or individual entities were in a position to bring their vested interests into the activities of the National Sojourners especially if facets of both were identical. As an example, the activities and pursuits of Major General Charles A. Willoughby, a Scottish Rite Mason, a member of the Shrine, and referred to as a "little Fascist" while on active duty, were researched from his U.S, Army retirement in 1951. The General started up the Foreign Intelligence Digest, (FID), at 3602 Massachusetts Ave, N.W., Washington, D.C. His Latin Affairs Editor, Emilio Nunez Portuondo, on November 17 ,1963, before six thousand people, gave a speech in which he bitterly attacked the UnitedStates according to a letter sent to Mr. James Rowley, U.S. Secret Service. Dec. 30,1963 and signed by John A. Marshal, Special Agent in Charge. Portuondo was the last Cuban prime minister under the dictator Batista who protected American interests in Cuba, including Mafia gambling casinos. Potuondo`s telephone number in the United States was traced for a message, overheared by a telephone operator, from Mexico City two Days after the Kennedy assassination. The message included conversation concerning the assassination. "*it resembled a report".*

In the early 1960`s , General Willoughby became a member of the Sovereign Order of Saint John of Jerusalem, Knights of Malta, which was also referred to as the Shickshinny Knights. Although goals and achievements were similar, the Masonic Knights of Malta and the Papal Knights of Malta were different, distinct entities. On Sept. 1, 1963 ,Willoughby acknowledged his designation as Chairman of Armed Services Committee with a roster which was a who`s who of U.S. retired military expertise, primarily generals, colonels,and admirals including Cardinal Francis T. Spellman, "*since they have nothing intrinsic to defend and no enemy is attacking them, who are they planning to attack".* Member Admiral Sir Barry Edward Domville, KBE., CB., CMG., was interned in prison in WW II from 1940 to 1943 because of his pro Nazi views, "*were they developing war games for the U.S. military, or arcade games".*

The Chancellor who appointed Willoughby ,Pichel, wrote to the General on Sept. 21, 1963 advising on information concerning Reds and Jews information supplied to Franco`s Spain; the General responded on Sept. 23,

1963, and again on Sept 26 ,1963, in which U. S. Army officers were discussed," ***officers of this rank do not fire weapons, they fire orders and words"*.Paul Mears Winter, Ph.D., was appointed by Willoughby to be his DeputySecurity General . In a response letter to General Willoughby, dated Sept. 4th, 1965, Paul Winters chastised the White House and Negroes with disgrace, "*was this a case of birds of a feather flock together"*. A letter from Dr. James A. Jacobs, O.S.J. was also received which compared the Shickshinny Knights of Malta with the Papal Knights of Malta, "*what is experienced as brotherhood protocol in a Blue Lodge may be a different brotherhood protocol outside the Blue Lodge.*"**

The senior generals and civil servants in close proximity to the National Sojourners, Inc. represented a potential lobbying or controlling influence, "*who lobbies who,who controls who*". After the Bay of Pigs fiasco, President Kennedy fired CIA Director Allen Dulles ,a Mason, and the CIA Deputy Director Charles Cabell, "*Allen Dulles got even when he was a member of the Warren Commission dominated by Masons"*.

General Maxwell Taylor, Chairman, Joint Chiefs of Staff, from 1962 to 1964 was admired by President Kennedy and his brother, Bobby: General Taylor admired them, especially Bobby who was structurally oriented compared to the President who looked at the infinity of masses of people. The general kept Joint Chiefs of Staff opinions on Viet Nam deceptively away from President Kennedy according to Wikipedia, the Free Encyclopedia. General Earl G. Wheeler was Chief of Staff, U.S. Army, from Oct. 1, 1962 until July2, 1964 and was cited as a 33d degree Mason on the Famous Freemasons website. Admiral George W. Anderson, Jr, Chief of Naval Operations from Aug 1,1961 until Aug. 1, 1963 was in charge of the naval blockage of Cuba in 1962. He disagreed with Secretary of Defense McNamara's decision on multiple naval operations and management which McNamara viewed as divided authority according to Time Magazine, May 17,1963.

McNamara conceived Anderson's behavior as mutiny and cut short his term as Chief of Naval Operations according to Wikipedia, the Free Encyclopedia. Admiral David McDonald was Chief of Naval Operations from Aug. 1,1963 until Aug 1, 1967.

General Curtis LeMay, Chief of Staff of the United States Air Force from 1961 to 1965, led bomber formations into combat in WW II. He became a Mason in Lakewood lodge, Lakewood, Ohio, a 32d degree Scottish Rite Mason in 1955 followed by the 33d degree in 1959. The perpetual cigar smoking general clashed repeatedly with General Taylor, McNamara, and Air Force Secretary Zuckert. During the 1962 Cuban missile crisis, Le May clashed with President Kennedy and McNamara when he argued for bombing the missile sites in Cuba opposed the naval blockade, and after the crisis argued that Cuba should be invaded anyway and called the peaceful resolution to the Cuban missile crisis,"the greatest defeat in our history", according to Wikipedia, the Free Encyclopedia, "*rumbles in the ranks*

included General LeMay's usurpation of the President's authority in declaring a certain DEFCON and by demanding that he be empowered, in addition to the President, to deploy and detonate nuclear bombs". **General LeMay was a strong advocate for desegregation.**

On October 11, 1963, President Kennedy approved National Security Memorandum No. 263 which required the withdrawal of 1,000 U.S. military personnel from Viet Nam by the end of 1963. The Memorandum was sent to The Secretary of State, The Secretary of Defense, and The Chairman of the Joints Chief of Staff, *"Who in Washigton, D. C.., didn't know of the Memorandum on November 22, 1963".*

General David M. Shoup, a Medal of Honor recipient , was Commandant of the Marine Corps from Jan. 1,1960 until Dec.31, 1963. In May 1966,after retirement, General Shoup said,

" I believe we had, and would, keep our dirty, bloody dollar, crooked finger out of the business of these nations so full of depressed, exploited people, they will arrive at a solution of their own. That they design and want, That they fight and work for. . . And not the American style which they do not want. Not one crammed down their throats by the American."

Except for General Shoup, Marine Corp Commandant, the military leaders were Cold War zealots according to Arthur Schlesenger in his book, "Robert Kennedy and his Time", *"how many other Secretaries of Defense will admit to a U.S. wars as a mistake".*

Masonic entities in close proximity, were potential impacts on the resultant actions of the National Sojourners, Inc. The Headquarters of the Supreme Council, Southern Jurisdiction, of the Ancient and Accepted Scottish Rite of Freemasons was located at 1733 Sixteenth Street, N.W., Washington, D.C.. The Supreme Council, an autonomous self perpetuating body ,of thirty three officers, possess administrative and voting powers not held by other members, *"what would a similar organization with total control of a nation be defined as".*

This Supreme Council elects its own members, amends its own statutes and laws, and writes its own rituals. Charters are issued for subordinate bodies in cities, called Valleys, of states, territories, or countries, called Orients. Charitable causes and efforts represented considerable efforts and results. This Headquarters also published the bimonthly Scottish Rite Journal in which articles appeared concerning: the installation of National Presidents of the National Sojourners, Inc.; the hosting of their third annual JROTC awards by the Scottish Rite Valley of D.C., and the local chapter of the National Sojourners; and Notes concerning

Throughout the National Sojourners Chapters, several historical and patriotic flag programs were developed: one in particular had a Scottish Rite genesis. A representative of the National Sojourners, Inc., Old Dominion Chapter No. 364, was asked to represent the Scottish Rite of Southern Jurisdiction in the lobbying effort for the Citizens Flag Alliance, Inc., and the

Constitutional Amendment to protect the flag. Supreme Councils do not interfere with, or meddle in, the private affairs or business matters of other Masonic Organizations according to the Crossed Swords Clarion, American Military Scottish Rite Bodies, Orient of Nato Bases, *"this is a case of who does the defining"*. In England and some other countries, the Grand Lodge of Blue Lodges does not accord official recognition to the Scottish Rite although there was no prohibition against a Freemason joining it according to Wikipedia, the Free Encyclopedia.

The National Sojourners, Inc located at 8301 East Boulevard, Alexandria , Virginia, was a nonprofit corporation. The non profit National Sojourners, Inc. parented the for profit National Sojourners Convention Corporation. National By-laws govern the activities of chartered Chapters and their Heroes of 76 Camps. The national fraternal organization claimed it met the needs of military Masons and advanced programs that promoted love of country. During war years, there were several hundred Chapters spread throughout the United States and overseas: recent listings showed seventy four existent Chapters, *"was there a chapter at the New Orleans Port of Embarkation in 1962-3"*. Sometime after the year 2000, the National Sojourners, Inc.. established criteria allowing senior noncommissioned officers to become members. The National Presidents forthe years 1962-1964 could not be ascertained through research. The National Commanders, Heroes of 76, were Lt. Richard Worthington, USN,1962-1963 and LTC Robert Lenhart,1963-1964.

Old Dominion Chapter # 364,in its September 2006 publication , cited itself as a nonprofit organization with Sgt. Ronald A. Dooley, Secretary. The only record found in the State Corporation Commission was for the parent organization, the National Sojourners, Inc. with Nelson O. Newcombe, Sec/Treas. The past presidents of Old Dominion Chapter # 364 were posted on their website for the years 1953 to 2007-2008, except for the years 1962-62,1962-63 and 1963-64. :the webmaster requested their names from anyone having their names. The Commanders, Heroes of 76, Old Dominion Chapter # 364 were, in1961-1962,Colonel Turner R. Sharp, USA , and in 1962-1963, Lt.Richard W. Worthington, USN. Both of the latter are deceased.

Circa 2006,in a discussion with a Brother Mason, who had a 33d degree, Stagner cited the Sojourner Resolution as a concern. Without denial of the Sojourner Resolution, the response was,

"Can't you leave that behind?"

Stagner replied, "I cannot leave it behind."

There was no shown interest in Stagner's cause for concern, *"the image of the whole was of greater priority than the Constitutional care of one,or many"*.

Several months later, a discussion with another Brother Mason,who had a 33d degree, was harmoniously reciprocal. Agreement was mutual on the members of the National Sojourners being good men. Stagner wanted to know what checks and balances were in place to preclude a repetition of the Sojourner Resolution, *"and the possible courts martial of some of those good*

***men for treason.*" Although the Brother indicated an effort ,Masonic entity boundaries understandably limited his scope of response to nil, "*and the Constitutional concerns remain*".**

February is a sunny ,warming month in the Tucson Valley. The golden globe sliding over the horizen pulls a darkening blanket up the shoulders of the muscular Santa Catalinas , sometimes preceded by a slender collar of fading pink. The days are getting longer and there is more light.

Convent of the Order
Shickshinny 2, Pa.

September 11 1959

Maj. Gen. Charles A. Willoughby,
3602 Massachusetts Ave., N.W., (Personal)
Washington, D. C.

Dear General:

Permit us to congratulate you upon your personal merit and patriotic career in being selected by our Board of Directors as one of 500 eminent Christian laymen in the U. S. best qualified to be considered a prospective Knight of our Order.

Not knowing if this event is of any interest to you, but awaiting your judgment, we are, most honored General,

Very respectfully,

Chas. L. T. Pichel, O.S.J.

P.S. Your name has been sponsored by Gen. Bonner Fellers and Russell Maguire, and others of our Order.

Mailed: McArthur 87 Documentation Same Date

Sept 1/ 63

The Hon Chas L. T. Pichel O.S.J.
The Grand Chancellor .Sovereign
Order of Saint John of Jerusalem
Shickshinny Pennsylvania

This is to acknowledge receipt of your designation of the Armed Services Committee of your Order. I shall be honoured to be of service. I am familiar with the tradition and ethical purposes of your Order. We have had some correspondesne on the subject of member ship. I regret that I did not pursue it more vigorously.

I have been engaged for some years in a time and nerve consuming publishing venture , the " Foreign Intelligence Digest " which I started in Washington ,in 1958 in order to contribute my specialized knowledge and experience in the field of intelligence, counter-intelligence and security surveillance. I expect to present certain data, under these headings, which fall in the purview of your " Security General ", at a later date.

In order that you may have a firm idea of my activities - alas, at seventy-one years of age, I am somewhat in a hurry ? ,I enlcose certain data, for your file and circulation amongst the Supreme Council, viz :

(1) New York Times Book Reveiw. Oct 3/ 1954.
(2) General MacArthur. Preface to " Intelligence Series".Sept 30/1950
(3) International Comité .Bonn. February 1963.
(4) Circular describing " Foreign Intelligence Digest ". 1963
(5) Sample article in the F.I.D. June 1963. (International)
(6) Ditto. July 1963 (Industrial)
(7) Partial List of articles, in various outlets.1952-1961.
(8) Desritpive Circular " Weekly Crusader".(Discontinued)
(9) Sample of Leaflet,(intermediary)on foreign intelligence
(10) Sampke of F.I.D. (semi political) Jan. 26/ 1962
(11) Ditto October 6/ 1961
(12) Circular " Legion of Honor". Biographical Record.

I invite your attention, also, to the fine print in upper right hand-corner, as a summation of personal and govermental service, as well as a digest of my literary and joruanlistic activities.

Under separate cover, I shall mail you copies of some of my books, for the Library of the Convent of the Order , viz : " MacArthur 1941- 1951 " (See enclosure (1) supra) and the " Partial Documentation of the Sorge Espionage Case " (a collector's item as the limited edit ion is in the hands of intelligence and security agencies, for training and

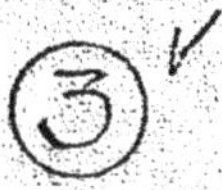

Specially qualified Knights selected by the Supreme Council to serve on the

ARMED SERVICES COMMITTEE

of the

SOVEREIGN ORDER OF SAINT JOHN OF JERUSALEM

General Lemuel C. Shepherd, USM. Ret., Leeton Forest, Warrenton, Virginia
Lieutenant General Pedro A. del Valle, USMC Ret., 41 Cornhill Rd., Annapolis, Md.
Lieutenant General Clovis E. Byers, USA Ret., 2801 29th Place, N.W., Wash. 8, D.C.
Major General Charles J. Willoughby, USA Ret., 3602 Mass. Ave., N.W., Wash. 7, D.C.
Major General Walter Allen DeLamater, USA Ret., Box 175, Rhinebeck, N. Y.
Major General Douglass Taft Greene, USA Ret., 835 Morgan Ave., Drexel Hill, Pa.
Brigadier General H. Terry Morrison, USA Ret., The Hermitage, Mound, Minn.
Brigadier General Bonner Fellers, USA Ret., 3535 Springland Lane, Wash. 8, D.C.
Brigadier General Edwin Cox, USA Ret., Aylett, Virginia
Brigadier General J. Harry LaBrum, USA Ret., 1830 N. 69th St., Phila. 31, Pa.
Lord Malcolm Douglas-Hamilton, OBE, DFC., RAF., Hewlett, N. Y. and London
Marquis de Amodio, CB., CBE., MC., former Squadron Leader, Pres. RACA. Paris
Colonel Philip J. Corso, USA Ret., 305 Leighton Drive, Falls Church, Virginia
Colonel Catesby ap Catesby Jones, USA Ret., 7 Ampthill Rd., Richmond 28, Va.
Colonel George Stewart, USAF., Ret., Dublin, New Hampshire
Colonel John Monroe Johnson, USA Ret., Suite 715, 1000 Conn. Ave., N.W., Wash. 6
Admiral Sir Barry Edward Domville, KBE., CB., CMG., Roehampton, London S.W. 15
Vice Admiral Harold Davies Baker, USN Ret., 2210 Wyoming Ave., N.W., Wash. 8, D.C.
Rear Admiral Arthur A. de la Houssaye, USN Ret., 1424 Richards Bldg., New Orleans
Rear Admiral Robert Lee Porter, USN Ret., 436 Parkview Drive, Wynnewood, Pa.
Rear Admiral Herbert S. Howard, USN. Ret., 2807 36th Place, Washington. 7, D.C.
Rear Admiral Richard Blackburn Black, USN Ret., Rippon Lodge, Woodbridge, Va.
Rear Admiral Francis T. Spellman, USN. Ret., 64 Thornton Rd., Chestnut Hill 67, Mass.
Rear Admiral Francis W. Benson, USN. Ret., 3117 28th St., San Diego 4, Calif.
Commodore Howard H. J. Benson, USN Ret., 114 Duke of Gloucester St., Annapolis, Md.

Purpose of Committee: The above Knights have been singled out for their brilliant and outstanding careers as Soldiers of Christ and Advocates of a Free World, to petition governments, senates and legislatures to cooperate with, recognize and respect the work and program of the Order.

OFFICERS OF THE SUPREME COUNCIL*

Grand-Master: His Most Eminent Highness Prince Crolian Edelen de Burgh. As the 72nd Grand-Master, H.M.E.H. descends from the family of the first three crusading Kings of Jerusalem, the Count of Boulogne and Ponthieu; Fulke of Anjou, King of Jerusalem; also four lines of descent from Rurik the Viking, including Saint Vladimir, Grand Duke of Kiev, the first Christian Czar of Russia, Vladimir I. (980-1016), also known as "Vladimir the Great." Ancestral knighthood in the Order dates from 1177 in the direct male line.

Grand Chancellor: Charles L. Thourot Pichel descends from the families of: The allodium barons of France; two of the first twelve Peers of France, and the 42nd Grand-Master, de l'Isle Adam.

Secretary of State: His Excellency Dr. Charles Habib Malik. President of the United Nations Security Council, 1953-54; President of the United Nations General Assembly, 1958-59; Minister of Foreign Affairs of Lebanon, 1956-58.

Under Secretary of State: Dr. Burleigh Cushing Rodick. Studied International Law under Judge John Bassett Moore, the first American Judge of the World Court; Professor of History, Political Science and International Law; author of "Doctrine of Necessity in International Law."

Grand Prior for Europe: The Rev. Dr. Gerard G. Shelley. Descends from the family of Sir Richard Shelley, Grand Prior for England, 1561.

Attorney General: Brigadier General J. Harry LaBrum; also Chief Justice of the Supreme Court of the Order.

Security General: Paul Mears Winter. Master of Ceremonies and Lecturer; President of the Law Enforcement League of Pennsylvania; Life Member of the International Police Association.

Associate Security General: Count Kyril de Rohan-Chandor. Descendant of the family of the 66th Grand-Master, Emmanuel de Rohan; Associate Chief of International Intelligence.

Prior of the Russian Langue: Prince Serge S. Troubetzkoy.

Prior of the German Langue: Hans Nordewin Baron von Koerber. Professor of Art, Culture and Linguistics.

Prior of France: Baron Raoul de Lavalette. Descends from the family of the 41st Grand-Master.

Physicist: Bernard Benjamin Blazes. Hereditary Grand Duke of Samogitia; Director of Nuclear Research and Development.

Council Member: John Sanderson du Mont. Descends from the family of the 48th Grand-Master, del Monte.

(*) The above list is incomplete and alternate members have been omitted.

Honorary Grand Admiral of the Order:
Admiral Sir Barry Domvile, R.N., Retired, K.B.E., C.B., C.M.G.

Ecclesiastical Tribunal

Roman Catholic Section: Grand Prelate, The Most Rev. Blaise S. Kurz, O.F.M., D.D.; [illegible]

Russian Orthodox Section: Coordinator, Prince Vassilchikov-Shismarev.

Old Roman Catholic Section: Coordinator, the Rev. Dr. Gerard G. Shelley.

(Other names and offices not released for publication)

HEREDITARY AND HISTORICAL CONTINUITY

Other officers and knights descend from the families of 15 former historical grand-masters of the Order.

The government of the Order is also advised and guided by the hereditary descendants of the Kings of Cyprus, de Lusignan; the House of Anjou, Emperors of Constantinople; the Kings of Aragon, Castile, Navarre; the Houses of Bourbon, Hapsburg, and the Romanov Emperors of Russia.

The Order includes sovereign prince descendants of the ancient Royal House of Aragon, the sovereign rights of which were confirmed September 16, 1860 by Francesco II., King of the Two Sicilies; again confirmed and adjudicated by the Court of Justice of Pistoia, Italy, June 5, 1964.

More than 340 members are hereditary descendants of royal and noble families of the early knights and hospitallers of the Order.

Many hereditary descendants of former families of historical Grand-Masters, Officers and Knights of these ancient and original Hospitallers have intentionally searched out and insisted upon affiliation with this Order and its membership. This fact alone serves as sufficient evidence, proof and international recognition that the Sovereign Order of Saint John of Jerusalem, herein identified, exists today as the one and only true Knight Order of world renown, established 1048 A.D. in Jerusalem.

Supreme Court of the Order

Chief Justice: J. Harry LaBrum, Brig.-Gen. U.S.A. Ret.; Associate Justices: Frank A. Pinola, former President Judge of Luzerne County, Pennsylvania; Lemuel C. Shepherd, General, U.S.M.C. Ret.; P. A. del Valle, Lt. General, U.S.M.C. Ret.; Albert J. Wilson, Q.C.

Hospital Board — Director: Countess Emilie de Rohan-Chandor; Grand Hospitallers: Kay Duer and Theodore R. Jackman; Hospitallers: Pramanik A. Satralker, M.D., Theodore L. Bates, John K. Williams and Dr. J. Robert Carroll.

Military Affairs Committee

*Gen. Lemuel C. Shepherd, Chairman

*Lt. Gen. P. A. del Valle	*Col. William A. Bennett, U.S.A.
*Lt. Gen. George E. Stratemeyer	*Lt. Col. Philip J. Corso
*Maj. Gen. Charles A. Willoughby	*Lt. Col. Matthew P. McKeon
*Maj. Gen. Ralph C. Smith	Lt. Col Charles A. Moran
*Maj. Gen. Walter A. DeLamater	Lt. Col. Tarlton Fleming Persons
*Brig. Gen. J. Harry LaBrum	**Admiral Charles M. Cooke
*Brig. Gen. Bonner Fellers	**Rear Adm. Robert Lee Porter
*Brig. Gen. John K. Williams	**Rear Adm. Arthur A. de la Houssaye
*Col. Catesby ap Catesby Jones	**Rear Adm. Herbert S. Howard
*Col. William M. Chapman	**Rear Adm. Richard B. Black
Col. C. Martin Spooner	**Rear Adm. Francis T. Spellman
Col. Floyd M. Johnson	**Rear Adm. Francis W. Benson
*Col. Benjamin F. von Stahl	**Rear Adm. Irvin J. Stephens, U.S.C.G.

(*) U.S.A. Retired (**) U.S.N. Retired

The above Committee functions with "ad hoc" sub-committees.

Confidential

Memo for the Chancellor : Sept 26th 63

(1) <u>Designation</u> of Priories etc. My reaction is that they should be establsihed by <u>countries</u> (langues) in order to accept psychologically the element of nationalism/ This will not deprive the designated " Priors", in the States as being"Deputies " and natural American-liaisons, a face-saving device. This has a direct bearing on item (2) and enclosurres

(2) <u>Marquès de Prat etc</u>. Our letters crossed. You will by now have recieved a recommendation. I have been in touch with the Marques, and have known him for years. del Valle met him in Spain, during the first session of the Accion Cristiana Ecumenica. Note back of my F.I.D. Circular : de Prat's outfit has been listed as one of my European editorial liaison. See special enclosure (inclduing your photostat)

(3) <u>Interesting</u> refusal :Byers was Eichelberger's Chief of Staff (8th Army in MacArthur's Area). A good staff officer etc. , bright, good personality but considered somewhat of a " politicaan " and " operator " . There are other and better men. I will feed you additional names (to the list yesterday)

Lieut.General Albert C Wedemeyer." Friends Advice " .Boyds/ Martla
* Major General Hugh J Casey. 1290 Ave of Americas.New York 19 N Y
* Brig. General Bonner Fellers .Suite 335 /1001 Conn Ave N W Washing
Major General Ralph C Smith. 1536 Dana Ave. Palo Alto. Cal.
Colonel Truman Smith. 1235 Mine Hill Road .Fairfield. Conn.
* Lieut.General Richard K Sutherland. 1235 Coral Way.Coral Gables.
* Lieut.Gen. George E Stratemeyer A.F. P.O. Box 424 Winter Park. Fla.
* Colonel Laurence E Bunker. 46 Chestnut Str. Wellesley Hills 82.
Colonel T. Sapia-Bosch. 2819-39th Str, N W Washington 7 D.C.

(*) All in MacArthur's command area.Sutherland : Chief of Staff. Stratemeyer. Chief of Air Force, Japan. etc.

(4) <u>Suggest Monday Oct 7th</u>. However, unless you have planned this trip a<u>nyway</u> , we could meet after my return from Europe ! We are doing pretty well in an exchange of written Memos ?

(5) <u>Certainly</u> : It is prudent <u>never</u> to displacce and " old-timer" with a newcomer.

(6) <u>Agreed</u>.Perhaps, I shall get you another copy of the " Partial Documentation Sorge " etc., <u>a rare item</u> also denoting that the Order is anti-Kremlin and anti-Communist <u>until</u> such time as these scoundredls give proof of their conversion (?) Re Hunt, I will try again.

(7) Same remarks as under (4) supra. However, I am keeping <u>Monday Oct 7th free for you</u> , appr 2 P.M. ?

(8) Examine commenst att to each group of papers which I retrun to you, for you file.

~~Confidential~~

Memo in duplicate to General C.A.W.
Sept. 21st.

Thanks for your numbered replies 1 to 14 of my memo to you.
Our emblem: There can be no criticism of this insignia. There were several such double eagle heads.
Grand Duke Wladimir: This man was approached several times to join us and I enclose one of his indirect replies for you. He prefers to sponsor a poor down and out refugee living in a Paris cellar and claiming to be the "Russia Grand Priory." So be it. He is stuck with this, but it does not discredit us, only he is in the wrong. His "recognition" by Franco can only be a courtesy recognition, nothing more. You can safely ignore him, unless you are SURE you can WIN him. If you can, and you think he is honest, I will authorize you to appoint him our GRAND-MASTER, pending a vote of our Supreme Council. Use your jusgment in this please. I will approve.
SPAIN: If you can get to Franco, you might show him that our Order has always been FOR him. I enclose letters from my friend, Franco's first U.S.Ambassador to the U.S. I constantly supplied Cardenas with info relative to the Reds, jews and Spain. He will vouch for this. He is now retired, but previously he was the head of the Diplomatic School for Franco. Meet him if you can. Remember me to him.
SOUTH AFRICA: Enclosed are replies showing how I supplied the Chief of State with valuable information at different occasions. Always I tried to persuade them to LEAVE the UN. They still hold on, I dont know why?
PORTUGAL: The same goes for this Chief of State as South Africa. They still hold on to UN, tho UN is crucifying them.
UN: As I see it now, we are wasting time trying to convince the common herd about what is going on. They do not care. I think we can accomplish much more if we WORK ON CHIEFS OF STATE directly, to GET OUT of UN. If we can induce only one or two to leave UN, others will fast follow, and the international control will be broken and the MONEY STOP coming in to them. Personally, I am insignificant when trying to persuade these chiefs of state A man of your rank would be seriously listened to, I am sure. HERE is our best field for SUCCESS. What do you think?
Confidentially, I have been nursing Portugal and South Africa, to prove that our Order, and not the Papal Order will help them. This goes for Spain. The Vatican has NEVER helped Portugal, Spain or South Africa, never. We do. Therefore, I have been preparing this "build up" so they might give us DIPLOMATIC RECOGNITION. I have not asked for it yet. This could be your part, if you will.
Any country that will give our Order a piece of TERRITORY with complete SOVEREIGNTY, we in turn will sign a MUTUAL SECURITY PACT, at once with them. In other words it could still be their territory but under our FLAG. In some cases this might be an advantage to a country. MUTUAL PROTECTION, etc.
EXILED ROYALTY; Your idea is good and I give you full authority to work on them if you wish. It must be in strict confidence without publicity.
MALTA: I am anxious to insinuate our Order to head up Malta when they get their independence. There are two newspapers on the Island, we can have the use of one of them "The Bulleton" as we wish. Already they print all we send them. I do not know HOW to write articles to prepare them for us. Could you make up such propaganda artivles, under a different name?
Thanks for your church explanation. It is perfect. Congratulations.
So glad to receive your coat-of-arms. Thanks. Thanks for the War Souvenir
Can you reserve a little time for me on the 7th and 8th? I hope.
Thanks for your great help. Please send me names of high brass I can write to join our Armed Services Comm. after they become Knights. Thanks. We may need about six to fill in those who refuse to function with us now.

Sincerely

Chas,

Memo for the Chanceller : Sept 23/ 63

I received your communications this morning (Monday) I postoned everything else and reply immediately, as attached

(1) I was entertained by him, in 1952 when I was in Spain on the invitation of Franco. I have known Franco since 1926- when I wrote a first article on him: " The Rear-Guard Action in Xauen " - an incident of the Spanish-Morrocon War 1923. Waldimir, recognized by Spain as"Altesse Royale " main ains a sort of diminutive Court, with a few old friends, a Chaplain, a Foreign Minister etc. etc You enclosed his " Manifesto". Maguire printed it in the Mercury Psychologically and histoircally, the man is indispensable ? We must try. His own " priory " etc. can be linked with Eletski in Californa as " American Deputy " or"Deputy for American Affairs ". What is Eletski relation to Waldimir ? He would be under bormal cicrumstances a natural channel to Waldairmir . I will ascertain reactions discreetly. It is , however, not determined that I go to Spain, at this moment. See other remarks elsewhere, with your papers which I retrurn.

(2) See comments on Russian correspondecne.

(3) See comments and enclosure to other correspondecne . Depending on how I get along with Jose Solis Ruiz, I may go to Spain. I annoyed at the incident of his Biography. I won't let these people get away with anything. I am as good as they are - and then some. However, I am in direct contact with Franco thru the Military Civil War group.I know them all. - My book (and conferegce text as instructroat the War College) " Maneuver in War " Stackpole. arrusbur 1939 contained the first impartial account of the Spansih Civil War 1936-1939 to appear here .

(4) I know Cardenas. I was also entertained by him in 1952- but these are no solid foundations for anything. However, there is a person, in Madrid, who is worthwhile (and effectuve) : Marquess de Prat de Nantouillet, Ambassador and former Chief of the Am erica Sect Foreign Office (when Martin Artaho was the Sec of State). These are contacts (though I dislike the wrod !) to explore carefully.

(5) Same remarks as on other correspondecne, att.

(6) rtugal : See enclosures. I will explore that area

(7) I agree , in general terms. Here again, ceaseless literary camapign against the present hoodlum memebership . How? Individual and boring letter writing ? Of course not - a high - level publication, newsletter or pmaphleteering of superior typographaicl make up. The quality, for example, of your stationery

(8) A letter, to that effect, plus printed evidecne to that e fect, in your house organ - and not any other way.

(9) The time is ripe : Then you would have natural heirs to your " langues " etc etc

(10) Malta : Important. Important. Psychologially iresistible. How can you reach them ? There must be Knights of Maltese families , old settlers etc. etc. Or all in the fold of the Roman Curia ?

(11) This must be explored. I would like to know more/ Again- if you had a house organ, editorial exchange would become natural and frutiful. It is the basis of my own relationship with European groups and papers. Same remarks for (12)

(13) Yes, let's fix it for Monday the 7th ?

(14) I will examine the field promtply.

(1)

Sovereign Order of Saint John of Jerusalem

Knights of Malta

Visit our Exhibit at the
New York World's Fair
1964-65

Convent of the Order
Shickshinny 2, Pa.

October 11, 1963

Lieut-Gen. Albert C. Wedemeyer,
Friends Advice,
Boyds, Maryland.

My dear General:

We very much regret that for some reason unknown to us, you resigned from our Order. Please, will you re-consider, and come back with us.

This week I visited both our Generals Willoughby and Shepherd in Washington, and they too, echo my sentiments, hoping you will return to us to help with your wisdom and advice in these unhappy times. General del Valle also hopes for your return. I visited him last Sunday in Annapolis. Since then General Stratemeyer has come in with us.

With every good wish for your health, I am,

Sincerely

Chas. L. T. Pichel, O.S.J.

P.S. Please send us a passport size photo so we may send you our official I.D.Card. Thanks. We ask your consent to act on our Armed Services Committee.

This letter has been circulated but Pichel never received a reply to it. Why? —Pichel—

Sovereign Order of Saint John of Jerusalem ®

✻ Knights of Malta ✻

Convent of the Order
Shickshinny 2, Pa.

782 Wyoming Ave.,Apt.1,
Kingston,Penna. 18704.
Sept. 4th,1965.

Major Gen.Charles A.Willoughby,USA,Ret.,
3602 Massachusetts Ave., N.W.,
Washington, D.C. 20037.

Dear Gen.Willoughby:

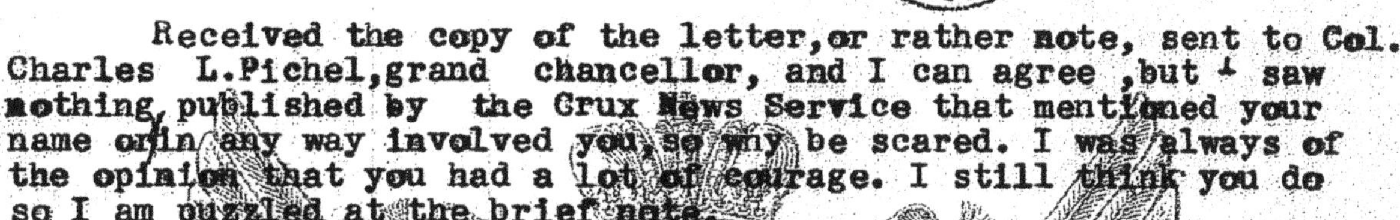

Received the copy of the letter,or rather note, sent to Col. Charles L.Pichel,grand chancellor, and I can agree ,but I saw nothing published by the Crux News Service that mentioned your name or in any way involved you, so why be scared. I was always of the opinion that you had a lot of courage. I still think you do so I am puzzled at the brief note.

However,I have learned that you have been rapidly recovering from your hospitalization and trust that you are feeling your self again. The tenure of the note would indicate that you are getting back your fighting spirit.

I am enclosing a brochure on the new coins, which are being minted by the S.O.J., and I might add that orders have been pouring from dealers all over the world requesting sets. Pichel has had only 5,000 sets minted and it appears that they will be sold out very promptly. It took $35,000. to have them minted and the Order will likely realize around $11,000. from the issue.

Edelen is back with us again and he finally discovered how crooked the other trouble-makers were and contacted Pichel. He has furnished us with a raft of information and evidence. It would appear that Jacobs has turned out to be a real rat and is sending out anonymous notes of a black-mail type. I think the postal authorities will be on his neck very quickly.

Recently read an article regarding the ceremonies incidental to the surrender of Japan on the battleship Missouri. I read that British officers got away with two of the pens used to sign the surrender terms, and that you obtained their return. How did you do it? It would be interesting to know.

My son,William I.Winter, who is with the Air Force has just been selected as one of 500 to make up the 1st Air Commando Wing, and he will leave for Vietnam on October 1st. You will likely read alot regarding this unit, as it is a real fighting force. I don't like to see my son become a member of anything involved in that racket in Vietnam. They use the M-16 rifle and must parachute.

You will likely be proud of Washington,D.C.when the negroes take over as they likely will when the city gets local autonomy. It is certainly a disgrace and one can place the blame nowhere,but at the door of the White House. At the heighth of the disgraceful insurrection in Los Angeles a captain of one of the airliners approaching the city addressed the passengers as follows:"The new Great Society is sending smoke signals to Washington, so we will detour the city." I thought that was very good and covered the situation properly.

Well, General, I have been wanting to write you and I hope your recovery will be complete. I just obtained a new member by the name of Chas.Henry Altmiller, who is worth millions. He has just been to Germany and he says it is a beehive and progressing in wonderful shape. He spent two months there. Gus Adler, commander of our barracks of the Veterans of World War 1, is in Germany with his wife and they will be there until October 20th. You met Adler when you were here.

With kind personal regards,I remain,

Yours for Christian culture.

Paul M.Winter,Ph.D.

I am enclosing also, a draft of an "ACT", which I prepared some years ago. I earnestly believe that this is our best answer, with the willing members of the Military Affairs Committee, plus myself, being "those persons" named as incorporators in "SECTION 1". I have in addition, a full set of "STATUTES" (BY-LAWS), drafted, based upon those of the British Order of St. John (640,00 members). As "senior man", General Shepperd, would be the ideal Grand Prior of such a group - and since it is "my baby" (and a "good-worker is essential), I propose myself as Secretary General (if necessary, at least "pro-tem").

With sentiments of esteem and kindest personal regards, I am,

Sincerely yours in Christ and St. John,

(Dr.) James A. Jacobs, O.S.J.
5313 Woodland Blvd.
Washington, D.C. 20021

P.S. Incidentally, I am one of the Roman Catholic members of Pichel's, gang. Entirely by personal preference - the difference between a minimum contribution and $1,000 "passage-money" and $200 "dues" per annum for the Papal Order.

cstampingr@dakotacom.net

From: "SccInfo" <SccInfo@scc.virginia.gov>
To: "'cstampingr@dakotacom.net'" <cstamping@dakotacom.net>
Sent: Monday, January 26, 2009 6:56 AM
Subject: RE: non profit

Only if the chapter incorporated would the SCC have such information.
Not for profit, tax exempt status is a designation earned from the IRS and the state tax department.

The only record I could find is of the parent organization, which is incorporated as a non-stock corporation. Typically, non stock entities are not for profit.

```
   CORP ID:   0216805                        - 2   STATUS: 00  ACTIVE
   CORP NAME: NATIONAL SOJOURNERS, INCORPORATED

 DATE OF CERTIFICATE:  04/22/1981 PERIOD OF DURATION:        INDUSTRY CODE: 00
 STATE OF INCORPORATION:  VA VIRGINIA      STOCK INDICATOR:  N NON-STOCK
 MERGER IND:                          CONVERSION/DOMESTICATION IND:
 GOOD STANDING IND: Y                 MONITOR INDICATOR:
 CHARTER FEE:            CASE NO:           CASE STATUS:    HEARING DTE:
    R/A NAME:   NELSON O. NEWCOMBE

      STREET:   8301 EAST BOULEVARD DRIVE                       AR RTN MAIL:

        CITY:   ALEXANDRIA              STATE :  VA  ZIP:   22308


                                                                 CURRENT AR# 2
 CORPORATE ID:   0216805                        2        0608 DATE 02/25/08
    CORP NAME:   NATIONAL SOJOURNERS, INCORPORATED

      STREET:   8301 EAST BOULEVARD DRIVE

        CITY:   ALEXANDRIA              STATE:  VA  ZIP:   22308
 S  C                                           DIR REQUIRED: Y
 E  A              OFFICERS/DIRECTORS DISPLAY FOR AR#  208-17-0608
 L  T                    NAME                              TITLE          SIGN
    O   JAMES E. VANN                                  NAT'L PRESIDENT
    O   NELSON O NEWCOMBE                              SEC/TREAS
    D   FRANK W HARRIS III                             DIRECTOR
    D   CLARENCE M NELSON                              DIRECTOR
    D   ELLIOTT B SAMUELS                              DIRECTOR
```

Kenneth J. Schrad
Director, Division of Information Resources
State Corporation Commission
PO Box 1197
Richmond, VA 23218
(804) 371-9141 (phone)
(804) 371-9211 (fax)

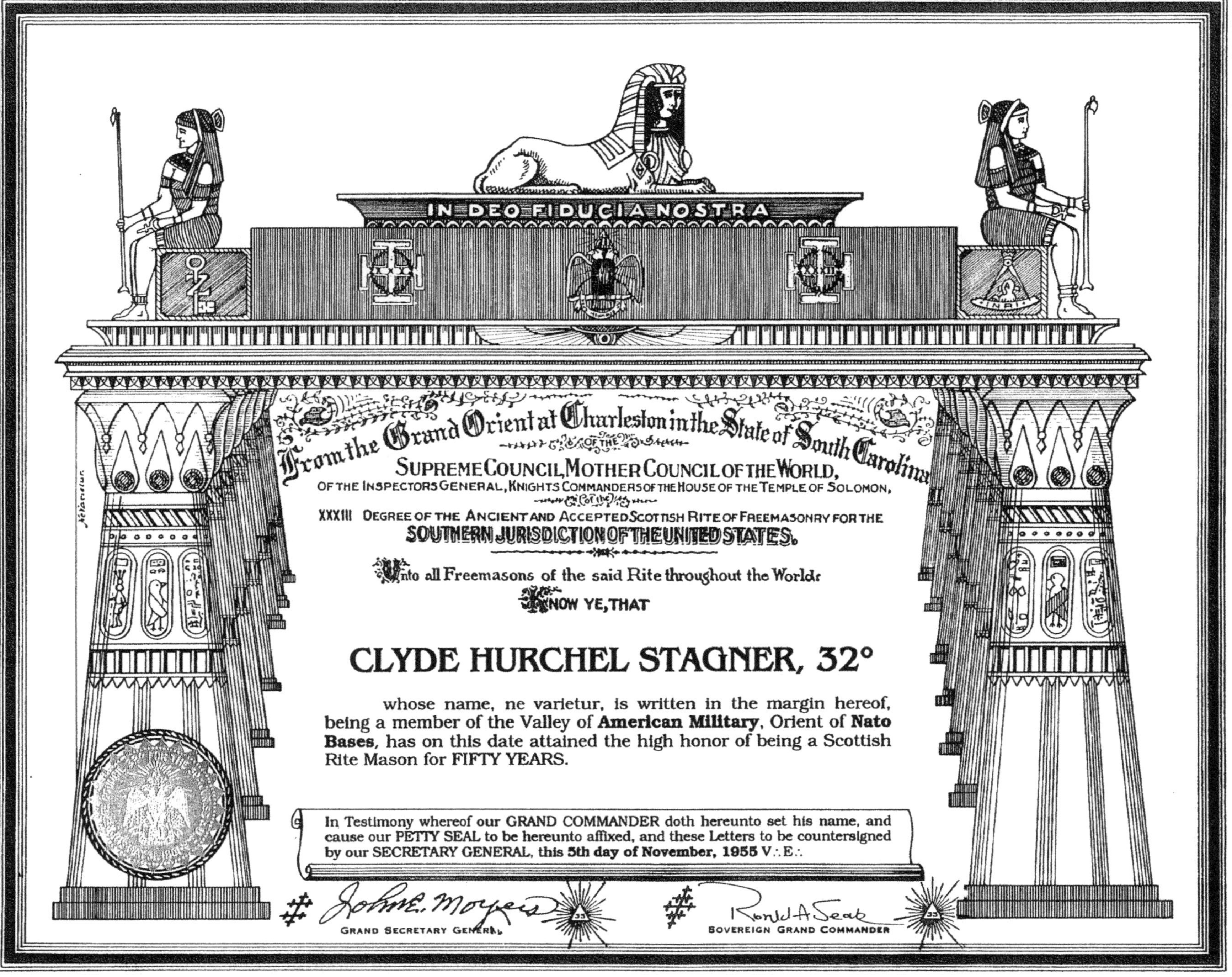

IN DEO FIDUCIA NOSTRA

From the Grand Orient at Charleston in the State of South Carolina

OF THE

SUPREME COUNCIL, MOTHER COUNCIL OF THE WORLD,

OF THE INSPECTORS GENERAL, KNIGHTS COMMANDERS OF THE HOUSE OF THE TEMPLE OF SOLOMON,

OF THE

XXXIII DEGREE OF THE ANCIENT AND ACCEPTED SCOTTISH RITE OF FREEMASONRY FOR THE

SOUTHERN JURISDICTION OF THE UNITED STATES.

Unto all Freemasons of the said Rite throughout the World:

KNOW YE, THAT

CLYDE HURCHEL STAGNER, 32°

whose name, ne varietur, is written in the margin hereof, being a member of the Valley of **American Military**, Orient of **Nato Bases**, has on this date attained the high honor of being a Scottish Rite Mason for FIFTY YEARS.

In Testimony whereof our GRAND COMMANDER doth hereunto set his name, and cause our PETTY SEAL to be hereunto affixed, and these Letters to be countersigned by our SECRETARY GENERAL, this **5th day of November, 1955** V∴E∴

John E. Moyers
GRAND SECRETARY GENERAL

Ronald A. Seale
SOVEREIGN GRAND COMMANDER

Scholarships for 2008:

Two scholarships of $1000 each were given to the American High School in Aviano, Italy. They were the only school to respond to our letter.

JROTC Award Program:

Our area of responsibility is for Twenty-five American High Schools located in Belgium, England, Germany, Italy, Netherlands and Spain. We sent the Scottish Rite JROTC Award packets to eight (8) American High Schools in Europe.

2009 Meeting Schedule

January 17th	Executive Meeting (all Masters) at 1045, regular meeting at 1100, Krupp Strasse 134, Frankfurt am Main.
February	**No Meeting**
March 21st	Executive Meeting (all Masters) at 1045, regular meeting at 1100, Krupp Strasse 134, Frankfurt am Main.
April	**No Meeting.**
May 16th	Executive Meeting (all Masters) at 1045, regular meeting at 1100, Krupp Strasse 134, Frankfurt am Main.
June 20th	**REUNION.** Executive Meeting (all Masters) at 0745, regular meeting at 0800, Krupp Strasse 134, Frankfurt am Main.

STRUCTURE OF THE SCOTTISH RITE

The Scottish Rite is an Appendant Masonic organization which administers a series of thirty-three degrees and bestows certain "Honours." It is active in every American state and enjoys a cooperative relationship with the American Grand Lodges from whom it solicits members.

The governing body of the Scottish Rite is the Supreme Council, an autonomous self-perpetuating body comprised of thirty-three officers, known as Sovereign Grand Inspectors General (S.G.I.G.), who possess administrative and voting powers not held by other members. Acting as a board of directors, the Supreme Council elects its own members, amends its own statutes and laws, and writes its own rituals. Supreme Councils do not interfere with or meddle in the private affairs or business matters of other Masonic Organizations. It is important to bear in mind that although Supreme Councils throughout the world are similar to each other, they may differ in minor aspects, dependent upon their adopted statutes.

For administrative purposes the Supreme Council divides the Scottish Rite into Orients which coterminous with individual American States, while overseas the Orients constitute an area of lawful jurisdiction (e.g. the NATO Bodies in Europe). Orients may be further divided into Valleys. A rough analogy may be to imagine the Supreme Council as a type of "National Grand Lodge"; the Orients as districts and the Valleys as constituent local lodges.

To save the Bodies money, we would like to distribute the News Letter's by E-mail. Please E-mail Ill. Bro. Glidewell at: amsrb.nato@pjsnet.com or Editor, Ill. Bro. Peterson at: ronpeterson@web.de

CPT Clyde H. Stagner (RET)
8565 E. Pembrook Dr.
Tucson, AZ 85715-4476

Dear CPT Clyde H. Stagner (RET):

America has always called upon the Army to do the hard jobs, and her Army has always answered the call. We are a free Nation, a Nation looked upon by billions of people around the world as the standard-bearer of freedoms -- freedoms guaranteed by our great Soldiers and by the veterans who have served our great country in the active Army, the Army National Guard and the Army Reserve.

We are an Army of tradition. Our greatest tradition is service to our country, and in that service we ask our Soldiers to carry out tough missions all around the world. Today, answering the Nation's call may take them into harm's way in our Global War on Terrorism, a war that touches us all and one that we must win.

As today's Soldiers serve, the traditions and legacy passed on by Army veterans in previous conflicts sustain them so they can do what must be done to protect our freedoms. Our Army would not be the best in the world without the service of its veterans who continue to provide support and exhibit patriotism. You make a difference to today's Army and to our country.

Please accept the enclosed Army lapel pin. It symbolizes the partnership between our Army, her Soldiers, their families, and veterans -- a partnership as old as the Nation itself. It is a partnership America has always been able to depend on. As our partner, we hope that you will wear this pin with pride, as a statement of our shared commitment to support America's Soldiers.

We thank you for the honor of your past service with our Army and for your continued support of our Soldiers.

Sincerely,

Peter J. Schoomaker
General, United States Army
Chief of Staff

Francis J. Harvey
Secretary of the Army

Certificate of Appreciation

is awarded to

CPT Clyde H. Stagner (RET)

For outstanding service to the Nation as a United States Army Soldier. You are being recognized for your patriotism and continued support of the Army family. Your legacy is today's Army and the values Soldiers exhibit while fighting the Global War on Terrorism. Their efforts are a direct reflection of your service, and the United States Army and a grateful Nation thank you.

Peter J. Schoomaker
General, United States Army
Chief of Staff

Francis J. Harvey
Secretary of the Army

CERTIFICATE OF DEMIT

Ancient Arabic Order of the Nobles of the Mystic Shrine

WHEREAS CLYDE STAGNER a Worthy Noble of the Mystic Shrine in good standing in Sabbar Temple, located in Tucson, AZ is hereby granted of Demit from said Temple and is recommended as a True and Worthy Noble to any Temple of the Imperial Council, Ancient Arabic Order of the Nobles of the Mystic Shrine.

SHRINE HISTORY

Name CLYDE STAGNER No. 4933

Home Address 8565 E PEMBROOK DR (Street)

City TUCSON County PIMA (Must be filled in)

State AZ Zip 85715-4476

Date of Creation 1/1/1983 Temple SABBAR

Number of Years Dues Paid ______

Permanent Cont. Member YES ____ NO ✓

Date of Purchase ______ Temple ______

MASONIC AND PERSONAL HISTORY

(To be completed by Noble when presenting demit for affiliation)

Member of ______ Lodge No. ______

Located at ______

Place of Birth ______ Date ______

Occupation or Profession ______

Address ______

City ______ State ______

Clyde Stagner

Signature of Noble

Witness our hands and seal of the Temple this 23rd day of October 20 08

[signature]

Illustrious Potentate

Glenn A. Davis, PP

Recorder

Nobles' Copy

Ancient and Accepted Scottish Rite of Freemasonry

For the Southern Jurisdiction of the United States of America:

DEMIT

This certifies that: American Military Lodge of Perfection
American Military Chapter of Rose Croix
American Military Council of Kadosh
American Military Consistory
of the Ancient and Accepted Scottish Rite of Freemasonry, sitting in the Valley of American Military, Orient of NATO, and of the obedience of the Supreme Council (Mother Council of the World) of the Inspectors General Knights Commanders of the House of the Temple of Solomon of the Thirty-third Degree of the Ancient and Accepted Scottish Rite of Freemasonry of the Southern Jurisdiction of the United States of American

NE VARIETUR

has issued this Demit to our

BROTHER CLYDE H. STAGNER

who received the Degrees as follows: 14° 06 NOV 55; 18° 06 NOV 55; 30° 06 NOV 55; 32° 06 NOV 55 in the American Military Bodies, and whose name, Ne Varietur, is written in the margin hereof, he having paid all dues and being in good and regular standing in the Bodies indicated above.

This Demit is issued at his own request and we recommend him to the fraternal consideration of all Brethren of the Ancient and Accepted Scottish Rite wherever found.

Given under our hands and the seal of said Bodies, this

15TH day of DECEMBER, 2008.

ATTEST:

General Secretary
AMERICAN MILITARY SCOTTISH RITE
ORIENT OF NATO

Secretary or Registrar

A.M.S.R.B., Krupp Strasse 134, 60388 Frankfurt am Main, Germany

U.S. Department of Justice

Office of Information and Privacy

Telephone: (202) 514-3642

Washington, D.C. 20530

JAN 21 2009

Mr. Clyde H. Stagner
8565 E. Pembrook Drive
Tucson, AZ 85715-4476

Re: Appeal No. 09-0713
Request No. 1123356
ADW:CGG

Dear Mr. Stagner:

You appealed from the action of the Headquarters Office of the Federal Bureau of Investigation on your request for access to records pertaining to yourself.

After carefully considering your appeal, I am affirming the FBI's action on your request. The FBI informed you that records that might have been responsive to your request were destroyed on October 1, 1987, pursuant to routine records retention schedules and departmental regulations. See 44 U.S.C. § 3302 (2000) and 36 C.F.R. § 1228 (2008). I have determined that the FBI's response was correct.

If you are dissatisfied with my action on your appeal, you may file a lawsuit in accordance with 5 U.S.C. § 552(a)(4)(B).

Sincerely,

Janice Galli McLeod
Associate Director

www.ingramcontent.com/pod-product-compliance
Ingram Content Group UK Ltd.
Pitfield, Milton Keynes, MK11 3LW, UK
UKHW061830190726
13855UKWH00005B/1741

9 781426 903106